What people are saying about …

Room for Doubt

"Ben Young has written a wonderful book for believers who struggle with doubt, and for doubters who struggle with faith. It is thoughtful and informed and honest and gracious. I recommend it without a doubt."

John Ortberg, senior pastor of Menlo Church and author of *All the Places to Go*

"Ben Young has written an honest book, one that can be given to Christians and non-Christians alike. It's a book about doubt, and he does all of us a favor by his willingness to talk about it. The apostle Paul showed courage when he spoke of his own despair, which came from an affliction beyond his own strength. Believers, even if they don't admit it, go through times of doubt. But Ben helps us see the ways in which doubt can actually be a vehicle for spiritual growth."

Dr. Robert B. Sloan, president of Houston Baptist University

"Through his personal story, the accounts of great heroes of Christian faith, and careful biblical exegesis, Ben Young shows us how we should welcome doubts and use our doubts to strengthen our faith in Jesus Christ and the reliability of the Bible. This book is the best I have read on how to process our doubts to develop a more secure and loving relationship with our Creator and Savior."

Hugh Ross, PhD, astronomer, pastor, and author of *Improbable Planet*

"*Room for Doubt* gives us a rare look at familiar men and women of faith from the Bible and Christian history who wrestled with doubt. Ben Young offers hope and grace for anyone and everyone who has serious questions about their faith. This is a must read for those struggling with doubt and for those who minister to them."

Marian Jordan Ellis, author of *Stand* and
founder of Redeemed Girl Ministries

"*Room for Doubt* is my new go-to book for any believer dealing with doubt. Ben Young writes with empathy, insight, and biblical truth. He offers practical help for those who want to do more than just 'survive' doubt but in fact want to thrive in the midst of it."

Gary Thomas, author of *Sacred Marriage*

"This book is pure gold. We all get lost in the forest of doubt from time to time, counting on some leftover cookie crumbs to follow. Ben Young has been there, and he shares his personal story with refreshing transparency. Within these pages is the map he used to navigate crushing doubt and find his way back to courageous faith. Whether you are a 'first responder' in ministry, encouraging a neighbor or friend, or on your own journey in the wilderness, this book provides the compass you need to return home."

Dr. Jay Strack, president and founder
of Student Leadership University

"From a very personal perspective, Ben Young sheds light on the fact that doubt isn't a bad thing; in fact, it's often the one thing that draws us closer to God. For anyone who has ever faced the foe of doubt, this book is for you!"

Ed Young, pastor of Fellowship Church and
author of *New York Times* bestseller *Sexperiment*

Room for Doubt

Room for Doubt

How Uncertainty Can Deepen Your Faith

Ben Young

ROOM FOR DOUBT
Published by David C Cook
4050 Lee Vance Drive
Colorado Springs, CO 80918 U.S.A.

David C Cook U.K., Kingsway Communications
Eastbourne, East Sussex BN23 6NT, England

LCCN 2017933745
ISBN 978-1-4347-1035-2
eISBN 978-1-4347-1045-1

Published in association with the literary agency of The Fedd Agency, Inc., Austin, TX.

The Team: Tim Peterson, Amy Konyndyk, Nick Lee,
James Hershberger, Jack Campbell, Susan Murdock
Cover Design: Jon Middel
Cover Photo: Getty Images

Printed in the United States of America
First Edition 2017

1 2 3 4 5 6 7 8 9 10

062917

To Jo Beth Young

Mom, you are the greatest Christian I've ever known. Thank you for always loving, always listening, and always lighting the way for us.

Contents

Acknowledgments

I want to thank my wife, Krissie, for believing in me and for believing in this book. Your editing and additions made this book what it is—no doubt about it! I love you immensely and cannot wait to see our redemption story unfold before us.

There were two people who caught the vision of this book from the get-go—Esther Fedorkevich and Tim Peterson. Thank you, Esther, Whitney Gossett, and the entire team at The Fedd Agency, for bringing this vision to life. I had the privilege of working with one of the best editors in the business, Tim Peterson, throughout the entire process. Tim, I truly appreciate your humility and expertise, which gave this book such depth and practicality.

I am grateful for Matt Lockhart, Annette Brickbealer, Chriscynethia Floyd, Jack Campbell, and the entire staff at David C Cook. Thank you for your hard work, expertise, patience, and encouragement through the process.

Toni Richmond has worked on all of my books over the years. Thank you for your unparalleled work ethic and servant's heart to help make this book a reality. Every day you make ministry happen on so many levels, *irregardless* of the challenges any week may bring.

A lot of the research for this book was birthed during my time at Bethel Seminary in San Diego. Justin Irving served as the director of the doctoral program, Don Reed was my dissertation adviser, and Terry Walling was the head coach of my cohort. Thank you for pouring your life and knowledge into me throughout those five years.

I am also indebted to the men and women who allowed me to interview them about their personal struggles with doubt. Your honesty and candor undergird the foundation of this work.

Cris Parrish has faithfully transcribed my sermons and books for years now. Thank you for working your fingers to the bone!

Tim Mavergeorge and Julia Prillaman are two talented therapists who helped me keep the faith through the dark valley. Your wisdom and kindness will never be forgotten.

And to the Jesus Bros: Bill Hill, Jimmy Seibert, Robert Hurley, Shawn Wilde, Sam Adams, and Dave Riggle (honorary JB), you were there when this story began. Your friendship and faithfulness through the years have been invaluable.

My dad's influence on my life is incalculable. Thanks, Dad, for your continual leadership, courage, and rock-solid faith. My brothers, Ed and Cliff, are two of the greatest guys on the planet. Thanks for your abiding friendship, love, and sense of humor.

And finally, I want to thank my wonderful daughters, Nicole and Claire. Girls, I love you with all my heart and soul. I am so very proud of you both! Don't forget to put on sunscreen.

Chapter 1

You Are Not Alone

"To deny, to believe, and to doubt absolutely—
this is for man what running is for a horse."
Blaise Pascal

Life is fragile. We desire security and certainty, but we often face a world full of unknowns, danger, and brokenness. Faith is also fragile. We yearn for absolutes and rock-solid assurances, but we often feel insecure and uncertain about what God is up to and why He seems to be taking so long.

Sometimes our faith needs to be broken in order to be found. Sometimes we need to walk through the dense forest of uncertainty and insecurity to find true security. Years ago, I found out just how vulnerable and insecure my faith was when I drifted into a turbulent sea of doubt and uncertainty. I felt alone and filled with fear.

I grew up in a conservative, loving, Christian home. I read the Bible daily, went to church on Sundays, evangelized my friends, and even put money in offering plates when they came down my row. I loved God. I believed in His Son, Jesus Christ, and I knew for certain that I would go to heaven when I died. I believed that the Bible was God's word without exception. However, during the last semester of my senior year in college, doubts crept into my head.

I had become involved in a church that made great claims about healing and God's supernatural intervention. I lived with five other guys in a house, and our sole purpose was to bring revival to our campus. Some people mockingly called us "the Jesus Bros." My roommates and I read various verses in the Bible about prayer and Christ's promises to answer our prayers in amazing ways. Jesus said, "The works I do, you shall do, and greater works than these will you do" (see John 14:12). It was simple logic. What works did Jesus do? He healed people. He cast out demons. He raised people from the dead. He said we would do those works and greater works if we had enough faith.

The guys and I took that verse literally and expected God to do mighty signs and wonders through us. We wanted to cast out demons, heal the sick, and raise people from the dead. We prayed. We fasted. We witnessed to people on the streets and even to telemarketers.

One of my roommates, Bill Hill, came home from class one day with a story about a car wreck he came upon. He could see the ambulance lights spinning near a severely mangled car and a bicycle on its side. Bodies lay on the ground. As he approached this tragedy, Bill thought, *This is our big chance to raise someone from the dead.* He was eager to pray for this miracle. But the closer he got to the accident scene, the more he noticed something. It wasn't real. It was only a simulation of an accident in order to teach students what to do in case of a real emergency. Bill was bummed. What a missed opportunity to perform a miracle for God and bring revival to our campus. That was the page we were on.

But we still tried. We prayed more. We fasted more. We helped the homeless. But nothing supernatural happened. No miracles. No healings. No one was raised from the dead.

After a while, we wondered, *Why doesn't God answer our prayers?* We fasted and prayed, but nothing happened. "Why doesn't God answer *our* prayers?" turned into "Why doesn't God answer *my* prayers?" which morphed into "Why doesn't God answer *any* prayer? Does God answer prayer *at all*? Does prayer do anything, or am I just talking to myself?" Perhaps my prayers just came out of my mouth, bounced off the ceiling, and hit me on the top of my head.

As I began to question God and whether He still performed miracles, my friends kept moving forward in their relationship with God. The apparent lack of answered prayer didn't seem to bother them. But at times, that seems to be the nature of doubt. It's often unique to the individual. In other words, some people begin to doubt God when their prayers are not answered while other people don't think a thing about it. They don't give God's silence a second thought.

During this time, one of my close friends was diagnosed with malignant brain tumors. He was young, athletic, and had so much life ahead of him. Despite the fervent prayers of our entire church, the cancer progressed, and a few days before Christmas, he died. After the funeral, some people just went on with their lives and their relationship with God, thinking, *Well, that must be God's will.* But I couldn't accept that. Why did he have to die at such a young age? Why did thousands of prayers go unanswered? Why did we even pray at all? Did God hear us, and if so, why didn't He answer? My faith was shaken.

At some point in our lives, most of us encounter a time of deep and intense doubt. Maybe yours is not about the existence of God and the reliability of Scripture. Perhaps your doubt is on a deeper level. You are not wondering if God is *there*—you want to know if God really *cares*. We sing and talk about the goodness and the love of God, but as you look at your life right now, perhaps you are saying, "God, I doubt whether You really care about what is going on. If You cared, You would help me. You would intervene in this situation. You would do something about the suffering that I am experiencing right now." It's hard to separate our personal circumstances from God's love for us.

But suffering doesn't have the same impact on everyone. Suffering can actually strengthen some people's faith while at the same time cause others to question why a loving God would *allow* such pain. One person may read a book like *The God Delusion* by Richard Dawkins and have their world rocked; another person may read the same book and find that it ends up strengthening their faith.

When it comes to doubt, there is no one size that fits all. Some people struggle with it, and some people don't. Some people scream their way into doubt through pain and suffering, and others seem to drift into it. For some of us, the doubt lasts for a few days; for others, months; and for some, years.

In my case, once my faith started to crack, doubts flooded my mind without mercy. I began to question everything. *Is God real? Is the Bible true? Is Jesus really God? What about all those other world religions? How can they be wrong? Why did Jesus go to Israel? Why not China where there were more people? What about hell? What does a man dying on a cross two thousand years ago have to do with me today? What about the contradictory reports of Judas's death and the number of angels at the resurrection? What about the resurrection? Did Jesus really come out of the grave alive from the dead, or was that a hoax? What about evolution? Is that a better explanation of how we got here?* Wave after wave of doubts pounded my mind. I felt like I couldn't breathe. I was drowning. I felt alone, sinking in a sea of doubts.

Different Ways We Come to Doubt

As time passed, I realized that I was not alone. I've since talked to many people who have been submerged in a sea of doubt just like I had. Unanswered prayer plunged me into a long struggle with uncertainty. I could not reconcile the promises of God's supernatural intervention with my personal experience of seeing zero intervention in my life and the lives of those around me. I felt like God overpromised and underdelivered. That's when my struggle began, but other factors can plunge people into a faith crisis as well. I want to share a story to show an example of a person who was thrust into doubt instead of drifting into it.

A friend of mine named Kevin grew up in a loving family and a peaceful home. When he was young, his father traveled constantly. Kevin was only eleven years old when his mother came to him in tears and told him that his dad had been murdered in a foreign country. Understandably, young Kevin was filled with anger. He went to the windowsill, took out a pocket knife, and carved the words "I hate God" into it. How could a loving God allow someone to kill his father? It didn't make any sense. This horrific, traumatic experience caused him to doubt the existence of God for many years.

I recently received a letter from a businessman who had grown up in the church. He was happily married with two kids, and his family was very active in their local church. However, he became interested in some of the popular books put out by the new atheists—Sam Harris, Christopher Hitchens, and Daniel Dennett. Their arguments against God captivated this dedicated Christian. After years of studying the works of these persuasive skeptics, along with a few Christians who attempted to refute them, he gave up his belief in God altogether.

Another reason we doubt is because we fuse our beliefs about our earthly father with those surrounding our heavenly Father.

I've seen this many times. The experiences we have as children are formative and powerful. We take the negative experiences we had of our earthly dad, and as we get older, we subconsciously project them onto our heavenly Father.

Years ago, I had a conversation with a professing atheist, and I remember asking him, "Why don't you believe in God?" He replied with the list of classic arguments: "Well, first of all, with so much evil and suffering in the world, how can anyone believe in God? If there is a God, He is not a good God. Second of all, look at science and evolution. Haven't they proven that the God of Scripture, the Christian God, is not true? We have no need for a deity anymore. And look at the great diversity of religions and pluralistic belief systems that we have today. I mean, are you really saying all these people are wrong and you're right? What about the people who have never heard this message? What is going to happen to them?"

After talking with him for a while about all these issues, I asked him, "Mike, what was it like growing up in your house?"

He said, "I never really knew my dad. When I was two years old, he left us." He went on to describe how his views of life and of love had been severely damaged by this abandonment.

His answer told the larger story. I responded, "Mike, I can help you find some answers to the questions you have about God and the Christian faith. By no means do I have all the answers, but I have some books that do. I know some people who have a lot more knowledge than I have, and I think they'll be able to answer your questions. But I believe, in the long run, you're going to see that your real reason for rejecting God and Christ is not any of the initial reasons you brought up. When your dad left you as a kid, somehow, in your heart and your mind, God left you too."

Dr. Paul Vitz is a professor of psychology at New York University. He wrote a book called *Faith of the Fatherless* that is a fascinating study of the psychology of atheism. If you look at the history of some of the most zealous atheists in the last 150 years, you'll see a common theme. Whether you are looking at Friedrich Nietzsche, Albert Camus, Jean-Paul Sartre, Bertrand Russell, or Madalyn Murray O'Hair, what you will find in almost every case is either a dead, a defective, or a disengaged dad.[1]

When we get older, we often have doubts about who God is and how He interacts with us because we are simply superimposing our earthly father's negative traits onto our heavenly Father.

Sometimes we fall into doubt because we forget to remember. Have you ever noticed that? It's easy to see the negative. But God has done many great things in our lives, and we forget to remember what God has done on our behalf. Forgetting God's faithfulness is a theme that runs throughout the Old Testament. There was an old hymn I sang as a child that said, "Here I raise my Ebenezer." I never understood that strange phrase until someone led me to 1 Samuel 7, where the prophet Samuel made an altar of stone (named Ebenezer) as a reminder that "the Lord has helped us this far" (see v. 12). A good practice is to sit down and write a list of "Ebenezers": those times when God intervened or did something real in your life. When we are drowning in an ocean of doubt, we need to go back and remember God's help in our past. When we only dwell on the more difficult side of life, we make room for doubt to creep in.

Stagnation is another reason we fall into doubt. We simply get to a place of complacency and stop growing: "Yeah, yeah, I understand the basics—I am just content to sort of sit here and kick my shoes off and relax at this level of faith." But when you reach that point and a storm hits your life, you are vulnerable to wavering.

Sometimes we doubt because no one took the time to address our questions. Maybe you grew up in a religious school. Perhaps you went to a church and had some legitimate questions about some things that you didn't understand, and the teacher or leader didn't take the time to really deal with your questions and give them honest responses.

I think about my friend Dana, who is now a clinical psychologist. When she began doubting in her teenage years, the leaders in her church had no idea how to address her questions. The standard answer came back: "Just believe," or "Just have faith." She felt marginalized when they failed to take her questions seriously.

I have talked to so many people through the years who had similar experiences. They felt like the church was a place for people with strong faith and not a place for people with real doubt. Maybe you feel that church is only a place for people who know all the answers rather than those who have questions.

There are all kinds of painful experiences that can lead to doubt: watching a loved one die of cancer, going through the agony of divorce, or having your faith seemingly dismantled by a professor who appears to be an expert on religious matters.

Doubt comes in all shapes, forms, and seasons of life. I believe that having doubts is not the problem but that it's how we process those doubts that really matters. In fact, I believe that some doubt is actually healthy and helpful. There is room for doubt in the life of faith.

Befriending Doubt

In my early days of doubt, it seemed to consume me like an addiction that was impossible to shake. It haunted me mercilessly for nearly a decade. It has taken me years to turn the tables on the power of doubt, and the game changer was seemingly counter-intuitive. In time, I actually learned to befriend and embrace the doubt. Now I believe my bout with doubt has strengthened my faith in God.

Alcoholics Anonymous (AA) has a slogan that says, "Only a drunk can help another drunk." I like that. Likewise, I believe in *most cases* that "only a doubter can help another doubter." Obviously, we can all gain wisdom from many places. At AA meetings, most people introduce themselves with this now almost cliché line: "My name is Bill, and I'm an alcoholic." I once heard someone introduce himself by saying, "My name is Bob, and I'm a grateful alcoholic." It sounded strange. But what Bob meant by this was that it was through his addiction that he discovered God and a better way to live life. Without the struggle, there would have been no life change for Bob, no vital spiritual experience.

After years of battling doubt, I can now say, "My name is Ben, and I'm a grateful doubt-aholic." Why? Because it was through doubt that I discovered real faith. It was through doubt that I discovered grace. It was through doubt that I gained a deeper respect for friends who do not believe in God and for those who see Him in a completely different way.

If you are struggling with doubt, I want you to know you have come to a safe place. Many Christians who are in a season of doubt fear being judged by family members, friends, and especially those in church leadership. Most doubters feel their entire world is caving in around them. This feeling comes from our growing fear that what we believed to be true all along may actually be a myth. This is a place of great psychological and spiritual pain. I experienced it for years. I believed I was a hypocrite for having all of those doubts. I doubted my salvation thousands of times. I felt the entire infrastructure of my life was crumbling to the ground.

A quick one-liner such as "Doubt your doubts and believe your beliefs" or "You've just got to believe" comes across as shallow and dismissive. There is some profound wisdom in those sayings, but it can take time for us to be able to process those words in a meaningful way.

Programs like Alcoholics Anonymous, GriefShare, and Divorce Recovery have been safe places for people to process addictions, loss, and relational pain. I hope this book will serve as a type of support group for you—a safe place to listen to others who share your doubts and who have come out on the other side.

My favorite philosopher is Søren Kierkegaard. I have found him difficult to read but easy to quote. One particular quote of his that has helped me overcome various challenges in my life is this one: "Life can only be understood backwards, but it must be lived forwards."[2] Looking back on my days of turmoil and darkness, I felt that my doubt would crush me. But at the same time, doubt challenged me, opened new doors for me, and in one sense, led me to a richer faith.

Once I began to speak openly about my own doubts, others began to confide in me about their own faith insecurities. I remember leaving a funeral one afternoon, and a woman came up to me and introduced herself. She said, "My name is Karen. I've never met you before, but about five years ago, you did a sermon on doubt. You talked about your own doubt and that helped me so much and I wanted to just say thank you." She felt so relieved that someone else, especially a pastor, actually struggled like she did. Having someone else to confide in is a healthy exercise and a necessary part of the process. Not speaking about your doubts can actually sabotage your faith.

It seems strange to admit that I feel qualified to write this book, and I do so for multiple reasons. I wrote my doctoral dissertation on doubt and conducted in-depth interviews with people who had gone through seasons of doubt. Some of the people I met with were still in a season of intense doubt. Some left the Christian faith, and some remained. Over time, I've amassed a large library of books on doubt. I've read volumes on the subject. I've spoken about it before thousands of people and one on one over a cup of coffee. But most importantly, I myself am a doubter. I battled doubt for nearly a decade, and I still go to war against doubt nearly every day. I've learned a lot through that struggle. And I've learned a lot through some great "Doctors of Doubt" like Os Guinness, Gary Habermas, and C. S. Lewis.

You Are Not Alone

I want to help you or someone you know deal with doubt. Here's one of the first steps: do not try to face your doubts alone. For years, I remained isolated and afraid to tell others about my doubts for fear of being judged. I felt alone and ashamed that I could have such continual doubts about God. If you take away only one thing from this book, I hope it is that you are not alone. You are not alone in your doubts. No matter how bizarre or persistent your doubts may be, you are not alone. Even though you may not believe in God at this moment, I know He believes in you. It is my desire to come alongside you and show you how doubt, uncertainty, and questioning can actually draw you closer to the heart of God.

At the same time, this book is not for lazy doubters. A lazy doubter is someone who read one book by a skeptic, watched some Neil deGrasse Tyson YouTube video, or heard a little of Bill Maher's cynical take on the world and now is smugly doubting or has left the faith altogether. That's lazy doubt with no real work of one's own. Now, on the other hand, if you are willing to drill down and get serious, then read on. If not, then just go your merry way. And as the biblical skeptic would say, "Eat, drink, and be merry, for tomorrow we die."

You Are Not the First to Doubt

Doubt has been around for a long time, perhaps since the dawn of time. We could travel to Athens and trace the history of doubt through Socrates, Plato, and Aristotle or begin with the doubters of the Hellenistic period: the Stoics, Epicureans, and Skeptics. Or we could jump into the Bible and see that it is full of men and women who had the audacity to doubt God. You will discover that many of the giants of our faith struggled with persistent doubts in their relationship with God as well.

Doubting is not unique to a person or a time period. It is the nature of being a finite human living in a complex world filled with pain, disappointment, and questions about existence that will never be answered on this side of life. Doubting is biblical, historical, and normal for many Christians who are trying to follow God with their lives. It takes courage to face uncertainty and to live with doubts that may never completely go away.

Justin Welby, the archbishop of Canterbury (which means he's like the pope of the entire Episcopal Church), recently admitted his own personal doubts. *The New York Times* reported, "He told an audience at Bristol Cathedral that there were moments where he wondered, 'Is there a God? Where is God?' Then, asked specifically if he harbored doubts, he responded, 'It is a really good question.'"[3] This authentic and vulnerable moment of coming clean was pounced upon by atheist reporters and Muslim scholars in the UK who publicly attacked the leader of the Church of England for making such an honest admission. On the other hand, millions of Christian doubters who have had similar thoughts were probably relieved by Welby's courageous statement of faith.

Awhile back, I was talking to a friend of mine about doubt and my struggles with it. He said, "Isn't doubt a cop-out? Isn't it easier to doubt than to have faith?" That phrase jarred me. I had never looked at doubt as a cop-out. My friend, who wouldn't even self-identify as a Christian, spoke some real truth to me. To be clear, I don't think all doubt is a cop-out by any means, but at the same time, to remain there forever without effort to resolve it could be an act of cowardice.

Existentialist philosopher Paul Tillich said it well, "Doubt is overcome … by courage. Courage does not deny that there is doubt, but it takes the doubt into itself as an expression of its own finitude. Courage does not need the safety of an unquestionable conviction. It includes the risk without which no creative life is possible."[4]

I'm glad you have the courage to walk with me through these pages of doubt, uncertainty, and faith. I believe you will make many new friends who share your depth of questioning, searching, and agonizing. I believe your faith can grow and become more alive. Author Jon Acuff said, "The scars you share become lighthouses for other people who are headed to the same rocks you hit."[5] The stories and insights you are about to discover are just a few of my scars that I hope will shed some light on the dark times you will encounter along the way.

So, this is the book nobody—especially not a Christian—wants to write. And not only a Christian, but a pastor. And not only a pastor, but the son of a pastor. This is a book about doubt. Really, it's about my doubt—my struggle with doubt and where it led me. But this is also a book about faith.

The other day I heard a story about a professor named Manfred Gutzke. A colleague I work with actually studied under him many years ago. Gutzke was a large, hulking man with a bald head and bushy eyebrows. He boxed in the Canadian army back in the day.

He began his teaching career in a one-room schoolhouse in a small Canadian farming town. Although he did not believe in the existence of God during those years and self-identified as an agnostic, he became particularly impressed by one farmer he observed in the small town.

This farmer went to church every Sunday and carried his Bible with him. He seemed humble and did not participate in the pre-worship-service gossip sessions outside the church. One year, this simple farmer sold two cows and gave the proceeds to the annual missions offering.

As he walked home from the schoolhouse one afternoon, Gutzke fell into a deep thought. *If God exists, then He can see me right now.* For some unknown reason, he took off his hat, perhaps as a sign of respect, I don't know.

Then he prayed: "God, I do not know whether You are there or not. And I don't mean anything bad by that. I just don't know. But I want to know, and You know that too. So please show me if You are real."

"I felt," he said, "as if something very important had happened."[6] And with that, Gutzke put his hat back on and made his way home. That was the turning point in this strong, tough guy's life. Gutzke eventually found his way home to God, became a professor, and taught other men how they could know this God in a deeper, and more profound, way.

If God exists, then He can see you right now. I invite you to take off your hat and ask God to make Himself real to you. There's a whole lot more to discover about the real meaning of doubt and faith, as we will see in the next chapter.

Chapter 2

Sliding on Ice

"Doubt does not in itself signify lack of faith. It may mean the opposite—that our faith is alive and growing. For faith implies not complacency but taking risks, not shutting ourselves off from the unknown but advancing boldly to meet it."[1]

Kallistos Ware

An Ice Storm, Not an Earthquake

I have never experienced an earthquake firsthand, but my friends from California have described to me what it feels like. The ground beneath you rumbles, and dishes rattle and crash to the floor. You feel unstable, and you have no idea how long the tremors will last or what will happen next. During a quake, the earth can shake so hard you may wonder if you are going to live to see another day. The whole ordeal can leave you off-balance and disoriented.

Doubt can be like an emotional and psychological quake. The foundation of your life feels like it is lurching to the left, then to the right, and you wonder if you are going to make it through. You feel unstable, confused. The faith you took for granted is no longer within your grasp.

When I drifted into a season of doubt, I felt as though my safe and secure world was quaking and crumbling before my eyes. God had been the foundation of my life and the constant source of my security and comfort. But when doubt began to chip away at that foundation, I started to believe that I was no longer a true follower of Christ.

I tried everything to rid myself of the doubt. I prayed. I got up early in the morning and cried out to God in the closet of my apartment, not sure if He was listening or whether He was even there. It was excruciating. My entire world was rocked. My certainty had disappeared.

Doubt was not acceptable, especially in the Christian circles where I lived. Doubting God meant you were a failure and probably weren't even saved. So I kept it all inside, stuffing it down in a secret, shameful place. I didn't tell anyone about my inner thoughts. But as bad as I felt about my doubts, my biggest "failure" was a gross misunderstanding of the nature of doubt and the nature of faith. At the time, the doubt I experienced felt like an earthquake, but I realize now that perhaps it was more like an ice storm. Let me explain.

Os Guinness uses ice as a fitting illustration for the nature of doubt. Imagine a small river that's been frozen over by a winter storm. You have a grassy bank on one side and a rocky bank on the other, with an iced-over river separating the two. If you crawled out onto the slippery ice, you would find that, in stumbling for your footing, you could slide between the two sides of the river. You could slide closer to the grassy bank or you could slide closer to the rocky bank.[2]

Doubt is like the ice between the two banks. The grassy bank represents belief, and the rocky bank symbolizes unbelief. Doubting is the place in between belief and unbelief. In a sense, doubt is neutral. It can slide you closer to belief or closer to unbelief. I made the mistake of assuming that doubt, especially living in doubt as I did, indicated unbelief. But that's simply not the case. Doubt is like ice. Ice is neutral. It can slide you closer to God or it can slide you farther away from Him.

If you ask people the question, "What is the opposite of love?" most of them will respond, "Hate." But hate is not the opposite of love. Indifference is. If you ask people, "What is the opposite of faith?" most of them will respond, "Doubt." I would suggest that the opposite of faith is not doubt; it is unbelief. Whether you are on the grassy bank of belief in God or the rocky bank of unbelief, you are in a secure and certain place. Your feet are planted on the ground of belief or unbelief. There is no instability or sliding around. But to be in doubt is to be in the middle between the two banks on the slippery surface of uncertainty. When you are on the ice of doubt, you can slide either way.

It Goes Both Ways

Two examples of the unpredictably slippery quality of doubt are the conversion story of Lee Strobel and the de-conversion story of Bart Ehrman. Strobel, a former reporter for the *Chicago Tribune* and the author of *The Case for Christ*, was an atheist at one time. What moved Strobel to believe in God, sliding him from atheism to theism, was doubt. He began to doubt his worldview. He began to doubt that naturalism and atheism were an adequate explanation of humanity's source, existence, and future.[3]

Conversely, the de-conversion story of Bart Ehrman, author of the book *Misquoting Jesus*, equally exemplifies the icy slipperiness of doubt. He was once an evangelical. He is now a skeptic. Ehrman was sold a bill of goods about the absolute perfection of the Bible.[4] He attended a conservative school that made great claims about the objective truthfulness of the Scriptures. Unfortunately, when he began to discover variances in the text, he panicked and eventually left the faith completely. The doubt he experienced had the opposite effect as it did for Strobel, sliding Ehrman away from belief in God and into unbelief and agnosticism.[5]

In both cases, doubt was at work. In one case, doubt slid Strobel toward belief in God. In the other case, doubt slid Ehrman away from God. Doubt similarly affected brothers

Christopher and Peter Hitchens. Christopher, an atheist, wrote the *New York Times* bestseller *God Is Not Great.*[6] Peter wrote *The Rage against God: How Atheism Led Me to Faith.*[7] Doubt led Christopher to slide away from belief in God to a fiery brand of atheism. Doubt first led Peter away from God, but then it slid him back to belief in God.

Many times, we view doubt as something that is always to be avoided, but that is not necessarily the case. Making room for doubt can lead people to faith in Christ. For someone to move from atheism to theism, it takes doubt. But at the same time, for someone to move from theism to atheism, it also takes doubt. Like unpredictable ice, doubt can move people in both directions. Daniel Taylor, in *The Skeptical Believer*, writes,

> Like tolerance, doubt is not in itself automatically a good or a bad thing. It is neither a virtue to doubt nor a virtue never to doubt. As usual, context is crucial. One must ask what is being doubted and in what spirit and with what result.... One feature of healthy doubt is a refusal to settle for lousy answers to good questions. One symptom of unhealthy doubt is paralysis. When doubt leaves you unable to commit or act in life, then you have a diseased, disabling form of doubt, not really a healthy questioning.[8]

So, according to Taylor, doubt can leave a person paralyzed and trapped in that in-between place, shivering and stumbling on the slippery ice—sort of like pitching a tent in the middle of the icy river—his faith frozen in certain limbo. But it can also push another person to fight for better answers. Taylor portrays doubt as neutral, neither good nor bad in and of itself, since it can both threaten destruction and catalyze creativity.

I know a little something about the unhealthy doubt Taylor refers to. I personally experienced many painful months where doubt immobilized me and I fell into what I call analysis paralysis. I would analyze my faith to death and entertain the possibilities of a variety of competing beliefs simultaneously, but I was stuck in a continual doom loop of analysis, doubt, and uncertainty. I could deconstruct all of my previously held beliefs about God easily, but I could not reconstruct a meaningful, coherent set of beliefs to replace them. A two-year-old can deconstruct his room in just a few minutes. Tearing down is the easy part. The more challenging job is to build something that will stand the test of time and have true worth.

Doubt Pushes You to Have Better Faith

Thankfully, at other times, my doubt pushed me to seek, question, and strive for better answers about my relationship with God and how He operates in this world. Doubt forced me not to settle for "Sunday school answers" and an inauthentic faith. Doubt introduced me to wonderful, thoughtful writers like C. S. Lewis, Søren Kierkegaard, and Blaise Pascal. When I read these giants of the faith, I realized that I was not alone in all my questioning and that doubt was a necessary component of authentic faith. And as we will discover later, any healthy definition of faith implies doubt in the first place.

I have spent close to thirty years studying, researching, and talking to people about doubt. Most of the time, I carry on an internal dialogue with myself in an attempt to understand this phenomenon that has been such a big part of my life. I have often wondered, why do we doubt anyway? Where does the tendency to doubt come from?

Original Doubt

Perhaps a good place to find an answer would be to start "in the beginning."

In the beginning, before the fall of humankind, it was doubt that played a key role in Eve believing the Serpent's lies over the truth of God. In Genesis 3:1, the Serpent said to Eve, "Did God really say, 'You must not eat from any tree in the garden'?" At this point in the story, Eve, and presumably Adam, had a decision to make. They had to decide whether they would trust in what God said about eating from the tree of the knowledge of good and evil or if they would believe what Satan said about

God's supposed dietary boundaries. Before Satan arrived on the scene, Adam and Eve appeared perfectly agreeable to eating from all the other trees in the garden, except for the tree of the knowledge of good and evil. It is not clear how long they continued to obey God in this way, but eventually they caved in to the lies of the Devil.

If we look closely at the history of original doubt with Adam and Eve, we can extract some very critical information. Although their doubt originated from an outside source, it appears that Adam and Eve had the preinstalled rational faculties to engage in doubt. At one point, they found themselves in between belief in God and belief in Satan. They had to choose whom they would trust. It seems this ability to ask questions, mentally or verbally, was placed inside of unfallen man and woman.

The DNA of Doubt

Too many times, we see doubt only as something sinful to be avoided. But theoretically and practically, doubt is not in and of itself necessarily a sinful activity. The capacity to doubt may be seen as a gift from God from the very beginning and a necessary part of human free will. The problem with human reasoning occurs when we attempt to use this "rationalistic impulse" to determine what is right and wrong independently from God's truth.

Two of Scripture's most famous gardens, Eden and Gethsemane, offer pictures of both the healthy and unhealthy effects of doubt. Doubt drove Adam and Eve to believe in Satan's lies in the Garden of Eden. But in Gethsemane, doubt drove Jesus Christ to lean into the Father's will when Christ prayed to remove the cup of suffering three times.

There are times when doubt can lead to sin—when it produces rebellion and unbelief. For this reason, the Bible does not encourage people to remain in a state of doubt. But as just described, the restlessness of doubt can spur creativity and even deeper faith. As Frederick Buechner put it, "If you don't have doubts, you're either kidding yourself or asleep. Doubts are the ants in the pants of faith. They keep it awake and moving."[9]

The difference seems to be what people do when they find themselves covered with ants or, to go back to our original analogy, on the slippery ice of doubt. Some cooperate with the slipperiness in such a way that they allow doubt to slide them farther from God. Others cooperate in such a way that they slide closer to God.

It was my misunderstanding the nature of doubt that led me into a multiplicity of errors, but it was also my misunderstanding of faith. I viewed faith as a state of mind where one could achieve absolute certainty about God, the Bible, and salvation.

Growing up in the church, I often heard preachers use the phrase "You've got to know that you know that you know." In other words, you had to be 100 percent certain that if you died right now you would go to heaven, and if you were not 100 percent certain, then you were quite certainly going to hell. The solution to this existential, eschatological quagmire was to "pray the sinner's prayer, and really mean it this time!" Or, in a dramatic and symbolic gesture, to pick up a nail and drive it into this wooden cross at the front of the altar. Or to pray the sinner's prayer over and over again, just to be sure. All of these techniques were designed to give the wavering believer absolute certainty about his or her salvation.

I am sure those methods worked for some people, but they did not work for me. Some days, I was 50 percent sure I would go to heaven. Other days, I was 75 percent sure, and some days, I was only about 5 percent sure. I always wanted to get back to that 100 percent mark but never could seem to muster up that kind of certainty again. I don't know if that type of assuredness is what God's looking for anyway. Our certainty must be grounded in Him, not in ourselves. I still don't have that degree of certainty, and I think that's okay.

Context Is King

Some of my confusion about certainty stemmed from a couple of passages in the Bible that really bothered me. James 1 and Hebrews 11 both sent chills over my faith. Bear with me while I try to explain this. In James's letter, it appears the author argues for a type of doubtless certainty that triggers the hand of God to give the believer what he is praying for:

> But if any of you lacks wisdom, let him ask of God, who gives to all generously and without reproach, and it will be given to him. But he must ask in faith without any doubting, for the one who doubts is like the surf of the sea, driven and tossed by the wind. For that man ought not to expect that he will receive anything from the Lord, being a double-minded man, unstable in all his ways. (James 1:5–8 NASB)

It would be easy to lift these verses right off the page and make a fairly strong case for certainty, or faith without a doubt as the means to receiving what you are asking from God. The "Word of Faith" movement is predicated on such verses. It emphasizes the believer's responsibility to have a positive confession of faith before going to God in prayer and asking Him for something.[10] The idea is that if you ask God to do something on your behalf, then you had better ask without a doubt and with complete certainty or else God will not answer that prayer. But is this really what the passage means?

A basic principle of biblical interpretation is that "context is king." This means that, when discerning the meaning of a passage in the Bible, you must read as much of the surrounding text as possible. In other words, you must always read the paragraphs before the passage and the paragraphs after the passage. As a matter of fact, scholar and philosopher Gregory Koukl believes this guiding principle is the single most practical skill he has learned as a Christian. He encourages people to "never read *a* Bible verse." What he means by this is to always consider the context. Don't read just one verse without first looking at the context of the passage within the specific chapter of a particular book. You ought to look within the context of the entire book. Then you should look within the context of the book's genre. After this, you ought to look within the context of the entire New Testament. Finally, you should look within the context of the Old Testament, and thus the entire scope of Scripture. But don't panic! You do not have to go through that multi-level exercise every time you read the Bible.

Gregory Boyd, in his excellent book *Benefit of the Doubt*, argues that if you read James 1:5–8 in context, it teaches the exact opposite of its interpretation by the Word of Faith movement. Boyd writes,

> To me, this broader context strongly suggests that the wavering James is talking about isn't concerned with doubt: it's rather concerned with whether disciples will rely on God for the kind of wisdom that will enable them to find joy in trials and to persevere in their faith to become mature and complete, on the one hand, or whether they'll be polluted with earthly wisdom that makes them "unstable in all they do," on the other.[11]

In this passage, James uses the Greek word *diakrino* to describe this type of wavering doubt. Boyd makes the case that James is referring to a type of wavering between loyalties, like a father who wants to see his son's ball game at six o'clock but whose boss is asking him to work late. The dad is wavering between loyalties.[12] Therefore, James is using this term to refer to wavering between seeking wisdom from God or seeking wisdom from the world when one is going through trials and various kinds of suffering. According to Boyd, he is not talking about some type of absolute, doubt-free certainty that will free the hand of God so that one can get whatever is desired in prayer. If context is king, this passage teaches the opposite of getting what one wants from God by maintaining absolute certainty in prayer requests. Rather, it speaks about how to receive wisdom from God when trying to endure intense persecution and suffering. It is in this sort of trial that James is exhorting his readers not to waiver between loyalties.

Another frequently misunderstood passage related to doubt is Hebrews 11:1–2: "Now faith is being sure of what we hope for and certain of what we do not see. This is what the ancients were commended for" (NIV). Some Christians believe that this passage provides an adequate definition of faith, that faith is being absolutely certain of what is not seen. The rest of Hebrews 11 unpacks what has been called "the Hall of Fame of Faith," filled with men and women who have overcome insurmountable odds by exercising this force called "faith." Just as with the James 1 passage, you could be led to believe that if you drum up enough psychological certainty in the invisible world where God dwells, you can also accomplish mighty feats of faith just like the people in the rest of Hebrews 11.

Dr. David K. Clark believes Hebrews 11:1–2 is a *description* of faith rather than a complete *definition* of faith. Not every statement of the form "A is B" is a definition. Some are merely descriptions. Dr. Clark uses the simple but profound analogy of trying to describe and define an automobile:

> If I said "a car is an object with glass windows"; that is a description but not a complete definition. A definition delineates the exact limits of some word or thing. It gives its exact nature. A definition is a description that differentiates the word from all others. Similarly, I could also say "a house is an object with glass windows." This statement about a house shows us clearly why the statement about the house and car are merely descriptions, and not sufficient to differentiate a car from a house or other objects. It is a description, but it is not a definition. A better way to define it would be "a car is a four-wheeled, motorized vehicle intended primarily for carrying passengers on roadways." This is a better definition of a car because it delineates a car in contrast to a house or all other objects in

> the world, while saying "a car is an object with glass windows" does not pass that test.[13]

A careful study of the context of Hebrews bears out Clark's argument. If "context is king," then, just as in the James passage, we must read the surrounding text of Hebrews 10:32–39 before we can properly understand chapter 11. This preceding passage shows that Hebrews 11:1 is an encouragement for believers to face suffering and uncertainty with confidence and strength. Clark says,

> Those who have faith will continue to look forward to what has been promised but not yet been given, even when persecution causes emotional stress and cognitive uncertainty. Those who have faith do expect to see something for which they have not yet found direct evidence. But this does not mean that this is the *meaning* of the word *faith.* This confident expectation is *characteristic* of those who do have faith.[14]

Faith Is a Relationship

Another way to look at biblical faith is more like marriage than a psychological mind trick. When two people are dating, they are each motivated through attraction to acquaint themselves with the other's character. Once they have gained enough evidence that they are a match, a proposal follows, and eventually, they are at the altar pledging their eternal love. As the couple grows in marriage, they get to know each other in a deeper and richer way, although they will never know each other completely and exhaustively. The same is true in a relationship with Christ. The essence of biblical faith is trusting in a person, the person of God as revealed in Jesus Christ. As the relationship grows, He is known more deeply and intimately, but knowledge of Him will always be incomplete and partial.

Though biblical faith does involve the mind, at the heart of faith is this trust relationship with the God who has revealed Himself to us in Jesus Christ. William Barclay says that "for Paul faith is always faith in a person. Faith is not the intellectual acceptance of a body of doctrine; faith is faith in a person."[15]

I believe that, to integrate doubt into a life of faith, you must appreciate the nuances of doubt and come to see it not as the opposite of faith but as a state of being in between belief and unbelief. Perhaps it would be helpful to see doubt as a neutral zone—like the icy country of Switzerland.

And while at times doubt may feel like an earthquake, it's really more like an ice storm. Although the ice can send us flailing into unbelief, the opposite can also be true. Finding ourselves slipping on the icy surface, we actually have the opportunity to slide into the open arms of the Father and deeper into a trusting faith in Him. Kallistos Ware writes, "Doubt does not in itself signify lack of faith. It may mean the opposite—that our faith is alive and growing. For faith implies not complacency but taking risks, not shutting ourselves off from the unknown but advancing boldly to meet it."[16]

For years, I suffered alone in my doubts. I thought doubt was the enemy and that the Bible was a book brimming over with people who never had a doubt about God in their entire lives. Boy, was I wrong. The Good Book is full of people just like me who weathered the ice storm of doubt. That is where we will pick up next.

Chapter 3

Throwing Dishes at God

"Christians seldom sing in the minor key. We fear the somber; we seem to hold sorrow in low-esteem. We seem predisposed to fear lament as a quick slide into doubt and despair; failing to see that doubt and despair are the dark soil that is necessary to grow confidence and joy."[1]

Dan Allender

My childhood was simple and somewhat sheltered. Our hometown of Canton, North Carolina, was a mill town of about five thousand people. The town was so small that it didn't have a hospital, and I was actually born in the neighboring metropolis of Waynesville. My parents like to tell the story of the time they took me to a Christmas tree farm when I was four years old. As we arrived at this magical place filled with rows and rows of perfect trees, my little self was overwhelmed with wonder. I gazed over the rolling hills of green, breathed the fresh mountain air into my lungs, and proclaimed with a smile, "This is God's beautiful world." I love that story. My mom has told it many times. Yet, something about that story haunts me to this day, over forty years later.

This snapshot memory not only represents the simplicity and calm of my childhood; it also represents the simplicity and certainty of my younger faith in God for nearly two decades. I believed that God's world was beautiful, that He sent His Son to die for me, and that everything in my life was going to play out in seamless, perfect, storybook fashion. However, that's not exactly how my life went. In fact, most people don't experience life wrapped up in a neat little package, like a present under a holiday tree. Most of us one day move away from home, wander into the far country, and long for the way things used to be.

I can't explain why life changes; I just know that it does. And change can be difficult to digest. French philosopher Paul Ricoeur understood the reality of change in the life of faith. He viewed life as a series of movements from orientation to disorientation to reorientation. When we feel "oriented," we feel like we are home. Things seem right, and there's a relative peace—"This is God's beautiful world." Home is where we desire to stay, but at some point in life, that sense of home is interrupted by some sort of life-altering event. That's when we move from a place of orientation to a place of disorientation. We long to get back to that place of orientation, that place called home where things felt so right, but we can't seem to find our way back. Ricoeur notes that, after some time passes, we reach a place of reorientation or relocation. We are not back home, life is different than before, but we are at peace with this new life, this reorientation.[2]

The truth is, nobody goes through life unscathed. Eventually, each of us will face a crisis, and it will feel like the world is crashing down on our head. When we are blindsided by disappointment, loss, or tragedy, our reality is shaken. Things are not the way they used to be, and we lose our sense of normalcy. When the sky really does fall and we experience this kind of "life-quake," if you will, many times we are pulled down into a season of doubt, disorientation, and despair.

One of the most gut-wrenching, raw stories of pain and suffering in the history of mankind is that of Job. His drama takes us on a wild ride from a place of orientation to disorientation to reorientation. Though generally the book of Job is summarized by its shocking beginning and its almost passive ending, the book is best interpreted in light of the middle section, the in-between time, when Job lays out his case before God and screams at a heaven that seems silent. The book of Job can be seen as a person's beginning faith or belief (orientation) in chapters 1–2, then the person's journey through doubt (disorientation) in chapters 3–30, and then belief again (reorientation) in chapters 31–42. Because he has come out on the other side of suffering, Job's belief is reoriented or modified. His view of God has changed.[3]

In this chapter, we will travel with Job through his rugged seasons of orientation (when life makes sense) to disorientation (when life doesn't make sense) and then to reorientation (when life makes sense again, but in a different way). I know when I battle seasons of doubt and despair, digging into the story of Job gives me an unusual hope.

Orientation—When Life Makes Sense

We first encounter Job living the good life in the land of Uz. We have no idea how old Job was during this time of "orientation," when life was good, but we do know this about him: He loved God passionately. He had a wonderful family with seven sons and three daughters. He ran a successful business, employed many workers, and had a net worth of about twenty million dollars, according to today's standards. The writer goes out of his way to describe how spiritual Job was. He worshipped God on a daily basis, prayed for his children, and was known as the most influential man in the land. Job was a titan of industry, a Forbes 500 kind of guy, and someone who would be called upon to speak at conferences on how to balance the demands of running a company, raising good kids, and following God all at the same time. I'm sure people came to Job for advice on how to pray, how to raise a family, and how to gain financial freedom. He was a guy who seemingly had it all. These were halcyon days for Job. He had his health, his wealth, his family, and most importantly, an authentic relationship with God.

If you are like most people, you can probably identify seasons in your life when God and His world made sense, when things were relatively calm and everything was going your way. Your relationships were stable, you loved God, you prayed daily, you were involved in your church. Your career was on track, you made the grade, and your health was good. Even Jesus Himself seemed to have a rather uneventful first half season of life, and that allowed Him to grow in wisdom and stature, and in favor with God and man. But we all know these peaceful days don't last forever. Tragedy and pain can strike without notice. And that's what happened to Job, as life thrust him into a season of disorientation and despair.

Disorientation—When Life Doesn't Make Sense

Within a brief period of time, Job lost everything. All ten of his children were killed, his business collapsed, and his body was stricken with sores from head to toe. All that remained was the air in his lungs and his bitter wife. Job fell into an extreme state of doubt and questioning of God as he tried to hold on to a mere thread of faith in light of the storm that had devastated his life. Job revealed how pain and suffering can cause even the most convinced believers to go into a tailspin of doubt and uncertainty.

But doubt wasn't his first reaction. Job's initial response to the devastation that fell upon him was remarkable:

> At this, Job got up and tore his robe and shaved his head. Then he fell to the ground in worship and said:
>
> "Naked I came from my mother's womb,
> and naked I will depart.
> The LORD gave and the LORD has taken away;
> may the name of the Lord be praised."
>
> In all this, Job did not sin by charging God with wrongdoing. (Job 1:20–22)

In the early stage of his great suffering, Job did not react like a stoic; instead, he mourned by tearing his robe, shaving his head, and falling to the ground in worship to proclaim the sovereignty of God in the midst of his pain.

His response was similar once he had lost his health and his wife implored him to curse God: "He replied, 'You are talking like a foolish woman. Shall we accept good from God, and not trouble?' In all this, Job did not sin in what he said" (Job 2:10).

Job did not charge Satan or himself for wrongdoing, but he painfully proclaimed his trust in God as the ultimate source of good and evil.

However, Job could not stay in this space of raw trust for long. In the third chapter, we see Job take his first shaky steps onto the ice of doubt. Verse 1 reads simply, "After this, Job opened his mouth and cursed the day of his birth." No one knows how long it took Job to slide from his rock-solid faith in God to the slippery and risky place of living in between belief and unbelief. The story does not reveal the timeline. What follows here are perhaps "the bleakest chapters in all of Scripture."[4]

From chapter 3 to chapter 30, Job unleashed a flood of complaints, laments, and doubts in the face of God. Three so-called friends appeared on the scene and attempted to explain to Job why he was suffering. The more his three friends blamed Job for his suffering, the more defiant Job became toward his friends and God. Job shouted out a death wish and cursed the day he was born. He asked God to take his life and charged God with oppressing him and approving of the wickedness that had befallen him. Job wailed, cried, and finally asked that God would just leave him alone because all of his hope in God had been destroyed.[5] Throughout this section of the story, Job shook his fist at God, demanding that he would have a day in court with Him so that he could defend his case against the Almighty (13:3). Job became frustrated as he cried out for an appointment with God and felt God responded to him with absolute silence (19:7; 30:20).

It seems we often ignore these middle chapters in Job (chapters 3–30), this horrific season of disorientation and despair, and skip to the part where God shows up, gives Job a lesson in cosmology, and everything appears to turn out okay.

Jennifer Michael Hecht, historian and author of *Doubt: A History*, put it this way:

> Certainly, one never dwells much on how this whole thing was a sort of careless bet with the devil. But even more than that, the idea that Job's questions about justice are never addressed, you know, the religious interpretations of this story just gloss over that and gloss over the rebellion and just say, "Look, Job was given many trials and in the end came back to God." And that's not the story as written. When you read the story, it seems to be much more a howl against the injustice of the world.[6]

In many ways, Hecht, though an atheist, is correct in her assessment. The middle section in this story, in which Job laments, questions, and "howls" against God, is often swept under the rug in some churches. I feel this "very human" section of the book of Job needs to be highlighted so we can know that it's okay to ask real questions to God. It's okay to doubt "out loud" when trying to endure intense suffering.

Recently, I watched a Bible study teacher in a local church admonish a Sunday school class for looking at Job as a negative book. He smiled and said, "Haven't you read the last chapter?" as if all the blessings God gave Job in the end somehow made up for the calamity that had wreaked havoc on his life. That didn't sit well with me.

Too many times, we try to put a Romans 8:28 Band-Aid on a Grand Canyon–sized wound. I've found that there are simply some tragedies that defy human attempts to make any sense of them. I frequently hear people say, "God works in mysterious ways," or offer the secular version of sovereignty: "I believe everything happens for a reason." My apologies, but I feel that such statements in the face of brutal pain and suffering are utterly meaningless. Of course, I believe that God does work in mysterious ways and that He is ultimately working all things together for His purpose, but raw suffering is real. Evil forces are real. The effect of the Fall on nature and mankind is real. The dark side of free will is real. I often say that we live in a broken, fallen world with broken, fallen people who do broken, fallen things.

Let's face it, on an ailing planet bursting with close to seven billion sinful people, we will inevitably face untold amounts of sadness, evil, and inexplicable pain until God brings this world back to a place of reorientation or re-creation. In the meantime, maybe we should trade in our glib catchphrases for some sincere empathy in response to suffering.

I have no idea why God does not intervene when little children suffer and die of cancer. I have no idea why God does not intervene when an anguished teen teeters on the edge of suicide. I have no idea why God did not intervene in the Holocaust while millions and millions of His chosen people were tortured, shot, gassed, raped, operated on without anesthesia, and had their skins stripped from their dead bodies to be used as lampshades. You cannot find a "reason" for that. Did He allow it? How can that make sense? If God is all loving, all knowing, and all powerful, how could He sit back and do nothing in the face of such horror? Do you think God loves the people who died in the Holocaust any less than He loves you?

We've already established that we live in a broken, fallen world. The natural world is broken, humanity is broken, and evil forces exacerbate this sense of brokenness. At the same time, God endowed us with this powerful yet potentially dangerous ability called free will. Most of the time, God allows our lives to flow in the stream of cause and effect fed by our free will. He does not always intervene on a personal level or a global level. In other words, He gives us the freedom to make our own choices: good or bad, productive or harmful, to ourselves or to others. Clearly, our free will can create whirlpools of trouble when we run into others' free will. Why He seems to allow things to spin out of control is beyond my understanding, but He does.

When you examine the perplexing, disturbing, and painful story of Job, all these kinds of questions surface: questions that concern the fairness of God, His nonresponse to Job's questions, and the purpose the Almighty had in mind to allow Job to endure so much tragedy and monumental loss. Think of the magnitude of what was stripped away. Job had to face what any parent knows is the most dreaded fear of all—the death of a child. Job faced this pain ten times over as he lost all ten of his precious children in one fell swoop. There is no greater loss than the death of one's child—the continual pain and suffering it brings is both incalculable and indescribable. No amount of salvation or good that comes from their deaths makes up for, justifies, or explains this tragedy. But somehow in the face of his devastation, Job's faith prevailed.

Reorientation—When Life Makes Sense Again, but in a Different Way

Job spends the better part of the book storming the gates of heaven, begging for an explanation for his suffering. But in the final chapter, he is mysteriously satisfied by God's non-answers to his questions and moves forward into a season of reorientation. Job is humbled by God's all-powerful and all-knowing nature and acknowledges his place as a mere mortal, one who is capable of only partial knowledge. Perhaps Job was simply overwhelmed by the "Godness" of God.

Jerry Sittser, who lived through an enormous amount of pain, said he was first repulsed by Job's story because of the randomness of his pain. But then he came to a deeper understanding:

> I also realize that Job stopped asking questions not because God was a bully but because Job finally beheld God's unfathomable greatness in his immediate experience.... Job ultimately found meaning in the ineffable presence of God, which he could not fully comprehend with his intellect but could only experience in the depths of his being.[7]

The story of Job instructs us on doubt in several ways. It reveals that, from the dawn of time, suffering has been and will be one of the major causes of doubt. Raw suffering, and the doubt that so often ensues, tends to be a polarizing experience; it produces both saints and skeptics. Somehow Job eventually embraced the necessity of paradox and contradiction in his relationship with God. Likewise, artist Stephen Shortridge explained:

> If I don't accept God's hand at work in the contradictions I experience, they're not mystery, just misery. In the midst of contradiction, I may be tempted to not trust God, but yielding to such temptation would throw me into the

> deception of trusting myself, whom I know better. Sure, uncertainty is uncomfortable, at best, but I suggest avoiding people who claim the ability to "clearly" explain the mysteries of God. They've clearly not met Him.[8]

It appears that Job chose to avoid his three friends, who thought they had the mystery of pain and suffering all figured out, and instead embraced the Mystery that is God Himself. Job ranted and railed against God for many chapters in this story and somehow slid out of his suffering in the direction of God.

I slid on the ice for many chapters of my own life. I thought I would never end up on the bank with a true faith in God. I thought I would freeze to death on the ice of perpetual questioning. Job poured out question after question that God never chose to answer. Yet his faith had grown so solid that, when God finally responded—and not with answers but with a rebuke—Job was mysteriously satisfied. I don't know about you, but I find great comfort in seeing here that God is big enough to handle the torrents of anger that Job brought against Him. Job doubted out loud. He cried. He raged. He chose to have an authentic relationship with God rather than live with stoic indifference or turn his back on God completely.

Job questioned, despaired, and demanded as he slid on the ice, raging against God. God never answered his questions, but God also never questioned his anger. And perhaps Job's "willingness to address God in his pain" or to "doubt out loud" gave him the courage to stay in the fight with God. In other words, even though he protested in his pain, Job ultimately stayed faithful in his relationship to God. Philosopher Peter Kreeft summarizes the status of their relationship at this stage:

> Job thinks God has let him down, so in a sense God has become nothing to him. That is a mistake, but Job at least knows it must be all or nothing. God is infinite love, and the opposite of love is not hate, but indifference. Job stays married to God and throws dishes at him; the three friends have a polite non-marriage, with separate bedrooms and separate vacations. The family that fights together stays together.[9]

I feel Job's main lesson was this: the Father gives us permission to doubt out loud when we are processing such deep and personal questions. If anyone has struggled to integrate doubt into a life of faith, it would be Job. He went kicking and screaming through his icy storm, but in the end, he came to know a bigger God than he ever imagined. If we are going to learn how to honestly and authentically process painful doubt into a life of faith, we need to rethink and reexperience the story of doubting Job, the man who threw dishes at God but continued to follow Him boldly.

We Have a Choice to Make When Pain and Suffering Strike Us

How pain and suffering shape us comes down to a choice. The following two stories reveal the choice we all have to make when we enter the crucible of pain and suffering, when we move from orientation to disorientation.

Many years ago, a young teenager watched a Billy Graham crusade on TV. He was enraptured by the evangelist's message and decided to turn his life over to Jesus Christ and become "born again." This young man continued to grow in his relationship with God and felt like he had a call from God to go into the mission field … until his sister developed a terminal disease that ate away at her body.

This committed Christian watched his sister slowly die. He began to doubt God. How could a loving God allow this to happen? It was during this season that his faith also slowly died. This young man went on to renounce his faith in God and became an atheist. This is the story of cable television billionaire Ted Turner.[10]

Turner's story is not unusual or rare. Many people doubt when pain and suffering engulf their lives. I mentioned Jerry Sittser earlier. Years ago, he was riding down the road with his wife, mom, and four small children. A drunk driver swerved into his lane and hit him head-on, killing his wife, his mother, and his four-year-old daughter. At the age of forty, Sittser lost nearly everything dear to him in a flash. He was left to raise three traumatized children alone. Not only that, but the drunk driver was later acquitted because of a careless error made by Sittser's attorney. The catastrophic loss he experienced made him flirt with the possibility that God may not exist after all. Pain plunged him into a season of doubt.

But unlike Ted Turner, Sittser processed his doubts differently and eventually penned an honest book called *A Grace Disguised: How the Soul Grows through Loss*. Over the years of helping hurting people, I had given this book to so many folks who were trying to cope with catastrophic loss. Little did I know that I would need this book to make it through my own season of darkness, doubt, and despair. I've read it about five times, underlining and highlighting nearly every page. Outside of the Bible, this book has influenced my life like none other. In it, Sittser carefully described how to maintain personal trust in God in the face of devastating loss. He revealed to me that we all experience some level of pain and anguish in our lives—that's inevitable—but the key to growing through that season is how we respond. He wrote, "Response involves the choices we make, the grace we receive, and ultimately the transformation we experience in the loss." He did not offer a quick-fix solution but pointed the way to a "lifelong journey of growth."[11]

Suffering polarizes people. It will slide one either closer to God or farther away from Him. It can be a disturbing, paradoxical "grace disguised" or a lethal injection resulting in unbelief. But we have the power to choose our response.

"Pain entered into, accepted, and owned can become poetry," wrote pastor and author Eugene Peterson.[12] I believe that doubt entered into, accepted, and owned can become poetry as well. We see that in Job. We, too, can have hope, an unusual hope like Job's, of emerging out of our trial of faith with a bigger God than we ever imagined. I know from experience that life can be brutal and inexplicably painful and that this pain can lead to a season of disorientation that feels never ending. But I also know this is still "God's beautiful world" and that He can transform this pain into poetry, a grace disguised.

Job's story of loss and how he processed it represents one of the major causes of doubt: suffering. But there are other reasons we often launch onto the ice of doubt as well. We will explore these in the following chapters.

Chapter 4

Demanding Evidence

"I will have nothing to do with a God who cares only occasionally. I need a God who is with us always, everywhere, in the deepest depths as well as the highest heights. It is when things go wrong, when good things do not happen, when our prayers seem to have been lost, that God is most present. We do not need the sheltering wings when things go smoothly. We are closest to God in the darkness, stumbling along blindly."[1]

Madeleine L'Engle

We all get to a point in our lives where we want more evidence. We want proof. *If I am going to bet my entire life on this, I want some solid evidence that God is really real.* On his ninetieth birthday, Bertrand Russell, renowned atheist and author of the book *Why I'm Not a Christian*, was asked by a friend at dinner, "What will you do, Bertie, if it turns out you're wrong? … I mean, what if—uh—when the time comes, you should meet Him? What will you say?" Russell replied, "Why, I should say, 'God, you gave us insufficient evidence.'"[2] He wanted more proof. He wanted more evidence that God was really real and that Christianity was the true expression of God. And atheists are not the only ones who wish God would provide more evidence of His existence.

Doubt of Biblical Proportions

Thomas is perhaps the most famous doubter in all of Scripture. When the disciples came to Thomas to tell him the good news that they had seen the Lord risen from the dead, Thomas reacted with skepticism: "Unless I see the nail marks in his hands and put my finger where the nails were, and put my hand into his side, I will not believe" (John 20:25). Thomas laid down his criteria for belief: he must first have concrete, physical evidence.

Think about this. The other disciples were amazed and elated that they had actually seen the risen Lord in the flesh! They gave Thomas their word that it was true and implored him to believe them. But the testimony of his closest friends wasn't enough. No amount of enthusiasm would convince him that Jesus was really alive. Thomas needed more proof. He could only believe if his own list of boxes got checked: *I want to see Him. I want to touch His wounds and see His hands and feet.* Thomas was full of doubt.

I often wonder why Thomas doubted. He had walked side by side with Jesus for three years. He had witnessed the blind see, the deaf hear, and the possessed delivered. Thomas saw Jesus walk on water and even helped pass the baskets as Jesus miraculously fed the five thousand. If those events weren't spectacular enough, Thomas had just had a ringside seat to watch Jesus raise a dead man from the grave! So why was it so difficult for Thomas to believe?

What is even more puzzling about his doubt is that Thomas did not hold an anti-supernatural bias. He had seen too many miracles with his own eyes for that to be the case. Despite the fact that he cried out for some empirical standards of evidence in order to slide from doubt to belief, he was not an advocate of an early form of philosophic naturalism. He was no Bertrand Russell.

We don't really know why Thomas held back and doubted, but clearly he did. He verbalized his doubt in front of his enthusiastic, resurrection-believing friends, thus earning the nickname "Doubting Thomas." I myself am glad that he did not keep his doubt a secret. If even this guy, who had lived life right alongside the Savior, could question, then maybe there is some safety out there on the ice for all of us.

Many years ago, my friend Beverly attended the University of South Carolina, where she signed up for a course called Christianity 101. When the professor walked into the room—we'll just call him Dr. Donald Jones, because that was his name—he wrote his name on the chalkboard. These were his opening words to the class that day in Christianity 101:

> My name is Dr. Donald Jones. I have received a PhD from Duke University. I am an ordained minister. However, I want you to know right off the bat, I do *not* believe in the virgin birth of Christ. I do *not* believe in the miracles of Christ. I do *not* believe in the bodily resurrection of Christ, and if any of you during this semester ever stands up in my classroom and says, "Let me tell you how my life has changed since Jesus came into my heart," then I am going to ask you to leave.

What an introduction! Coincidentally, when I was in college, the same thing happened to me. I had an Old Testament professor who tried to explain away every single miracle that was in the Old Testament, and probably in the New Testament as well.

Your faith can be challenged from any area of your life. Whether you are in college, the workplace, or the gym, or you are engaged in different conversations in the marketplace, you may be challenged, and you may find yourself ill prepared to deal with the questions. What does that do? It can cause *you* to doubt—and that can cause *you* to wonder, "Is what I am believing in—is that *really* true? Should I really bank my entire life on it?"

Even John the Baptist fell into similar doubts. When he was in prison awaiting his execution, he began to have doubts about God's love for him and the power of Jesus to save. He sent his disciples to ask Jesus if He was really the Messiah. Now, think about this. According to Scripture, John the Baptist was assigned a unique purpose in life, which was to point out the Messiah and prepare the way. He was even family—the cousin of Jesus. Earlier in his ministry, he declared, "Behold, the Lamb of God, who takes away the sin of the world" (John 1:29 ESV) and "He must increase, but I must decrease" (John 3:30 ESV). He proclaimed the preexistence of Christ when the preexistence of Christ wasn't cool (see the prologue to John's gospel). John the Baptist was a man of certainty. He possessed inside knowledge. God designed him to usher in the long-awaited Messiah. But now, as he found himself in a different context, isolated from friends and family, facing his impending death … he doubted.

He desired more evidence. John wanted to be sure, "to know that you know that you know." John questioned. "Are You the One? Maybe You are the One and maybe You are not the One. Can You give me some evidence that You are the One? Objective evidence that will settle our questions once and for all." Bertrand wanted more evidence. Thomas wanted more evidence. John wanted more evidence.

Most of us will never find ourselves in a jail cell like John, but we can relate to feeling isolated and detached from the familiar.

Moving to a new town, going off to college, going through a divorce, or losing a lifelong friendship can leave us disoriented. When we are separated from family and a believing community, we can fall prey to skeptics who question our faith, and doubts can arise in us, just as they did in John.

In my season of doubt, I desired objective evidence as well. I always believed that the Bible was God's word. It was all true. The miracles of the parting of the Red Sea and Jesus turning water into wine were literally true. I never doubted the supernatural accounts I read in the Scriptures.

This belief led me to start looking for miracles in my own life, as I mentioned—healings, deliverance, and raising someone from the dead. I felt like my logic was sound—Jesus promised us that we would perform miracles and do even greater works. The disciple Mark said signs and wonders would accompany those who believed. You can move mountains with faith. When these miracles failed to materialize, though, I began to doubt if they were possible.

In my final year of college, my roommates and I wanted to see these miracles, so we looked for them, prayed for them, and fasted for them. When they failed to materialize, I eventually began to doubt the power of prayer and the power of God altogether. That was the catalyzing event that slid me into a season of major-league doubt. Looking back on those doubts, I can now see how immature and petty my demanding a miracle from God was. I made prayer itself more powerful than God.

But during this time of doubt, I still wanted God to send some sign or wonder to bring me back to a place of peaceful trust. I was hoping to see just one healing, one demonstration of His power that would wipe away all of my doubts and questions. I yearned to discover any shred of evidence that proved God still intervened today.

One day, I stumbled into a Christian bookstore and bought a copy of a book entitled *Answers to Prayer* by George Müller. It was simply an account of all the many answers to prayer received over the years as he built orphanages by simply trusting in God to meet his needs. Müller lived in the 1800s before all the so-called faith healers came on the scene in the following century. God did not seem to answer *my* prayers, but at least He had answered Müller's prayers. Since my faith was too flimsy to sustain me, I leeched off his faith and relationship with God. The undeniable answers to prayers he received provided some evidence for my faltering faith and gave me some hope, but it was not enough. I wanted more.

Just reading how God supernaturally provided food and clothing for Müller's orphans gave me a ray of hope, a crumb of faith. God did not provide for me in inexplicable ways, but I had zero doubt that He had done so for Müller. I remember a particular story when one of his orphanages ran out of food for the three hundred kids living there. The staff housemother was greatly concerned and came to Müller. His response was to have them all sit at the table, to thank God for the food (which was nowhere in sight), and to wait. Very soon after, a baker came and knocked on the door. "Mr. Müller," he said, "last night I could not sleep. Somehow I knew that you would need bread this morning. I got up and baked three batches for you. I will bring it in."[3]

Soon afterward, a milkman knocked on the door. The wheel of his cart had broken in front of the orphanage, so he offered ten large cans of milk for the orphans that otherwise would spoil by the time he got the wheel fixed. That's unbelievable! And that's just one of many stories in Müller's prayer journals. George Müller was a very rational, logical person. He simply trusted God.

I copied his pattern of prayer in my own life. He would read the Bible on his knees and pray as he read Scripture. He would take long walks to pray and meditate on the Bible. I did those things as well. I started to read the Bible on my knees and go on long prayer walks outside of my apartment in the mornings. Like Müller, I would meditate on the reality that I was forgiven, a child of God, and a son of the King. I hoped that by following his example, I could reboot my faith and certainty.

After I realized God wasn't going to do a miracle for me to prove His existence and the veracity of the Christian faith, I plunged myself into trying to find a rational case for my beliefs. I volunteered to work in Amsterdam for Youth with a Mission (known to most simply as YWAM) for half a summer. I was still struggling greatly with doubt and skepticism, but another part of me wanted to push my faith to the limit and try to evangelize a pagan city. I witnessed on street corners, brought my Bible into bars, and even performed in dramatic gospel presentations near Central Station in the heart of the city. Imagine a flash mob singing and dancing and declaring Christ, and I was right in the middle of it. I worked with fellow Christians from England, Germany, Ireland, Africa, Canada, Sweden, Norway, the Philippines, and Egypt. It was amazing to be a part of such an eclectic group of people from around the world who were passionate about telling others about Jesus. However, the residents and many tourists in Amsterdam were not so passionate about receiving that message. I had numerous conversations with skeptics who were filled with doubts and questions.

Knowing my own faith was depleted and I needed better equipment to tackle the arguments these antagonists were throwing at me, I read an apologetic book by Josh McDowell entitled *Evidence for the Resurrection*. McDowell, a former atheist, converted to the Christian faith when he began to investigate the evidence for and against the bodily resurrection of Jesus. He also wrote *Evidence That Demands a Verdict*, which sold millions of copies worldwide. I used many of the arguments and threads of evidence presented in McDowell's books during my street-witnessing encounters in Holland.[4] But for all my study and effort, I saw bleak results. I won arguments and defended the faith with vigor, but no one responded to my presentations.

I think about my friend Glenn Lucke, who worked at a campus ministry at Harvard University for many years. Glenn, a former skeptic and outspoken critic of Christianity, came to know Christ while he was a student at Dartmouth. He went on to earn a master's in theology and a PhD in sociology from the University of Virginia. He was also well versed in presenting evidence for God's existence, the truthfulness of the Bible, and the resurrection of Jesus Christ. On many occasions after presenting all this evidence, students would agree with Glenn that his case for Christ and the Bible was rock solid. But then he said they would simply shrug their shoulders, as if to say, "Hmm, that's interesting and I'm happy that works for you, but I just don't care that much." Glenn often used *Evidence That Demands a Verdict* in his dialogues with skeptics, but he confessed to me he felt like retitling it *Evidence That Demands a Shrug*.

I am not against presenting arguments and evidence for the Christian faith. I wrote an entire book on the subject and know that for some people the evidence tipped them over the edge to believe in Christ or helped them put their doubts to rest.

In my case, absorbing the various rational, archaeological, and philosophical evidence for the Christian faith did temper my doubts on some level. But the doubts still lingered. I desired an airtight, objective case that no one could combat, but that case eluded me. Would God provide more evidence for me? How much evidence was enough?

I also felt ashamed for allowing these doubts to dominate my thoughts throughout the day. I kept my nagging doubts a secret for fear of being kicked out of the club or judged for not having enough faith. I simply could not shake them. I even walked the aisle of a Pentecostal church in an attempt to have the pastor cast out the "demon of doubt." Surprisingly, no question marks came flying out of my body when I went down to the altar. Nothing worked.

It comforted me to know that great men of faith like John the Baptist and Thomas doubted and desired more evidence to buttress their flagging faith as well. Because of their unique historical context, they received extraordinary evidence that only a few people were privy to. When John the Baptist voiced his request for more evidence that Jesus was the Messiah, Jesus relayed a message to him in prison: "Go back and report to John what you hear and see: The blind receive sight, the lame walk, those who have leprosy are cleansed, the deaf hear, the dead are raised, and the good news is proclaimed to the poor. Blessed is anyone who does not stumble on account of me" (Matthew 11:4–6).

It's as if He said to John, "Don't doubt in the dark what you believed in the light."[5] He reminded His dear friend John the Baptist what he already knew. He instructed John to ground his faith in various supernatural healings flowing from the life of Jesus. Jesus went on to say that no man born of a woman was greater than John. Did you hear that? Jesus did not condemn John for his doubts. He understood the brutal reality that John faced in prison and the inner turmoil it produced. He affirmed John as a great man, a man of strong faith, even while he was still doubting.

I felt so ashamed when doubt infested my life. I felt like a loser and a man of weak faith. I knew that people looked up to me as a mature believer, but now that was over. My doubts had swiped away my Christian maturity card. If I only had let the story of John the Baptist sink deep into my heart and mind at that time. If I only had known that even radical followers of Christ desired evidence at one time or another, perhaps I wouldn't have panicked so much when doubts engulfed me.

Thomas threw down even harder with his doubts and demanded tangible evidence to confirm his friends' story that Jesus was alive from the dead. One week following Jesus's first appearance to the disciples, He appeared to them again, in the same room, and the doors were locked. This time "Thomas was with them … Jesus came and stood among them and said, 'Peace be with you!' Then he said to Thomas, 'Put your finger here; see my hands. Reach out your hand and put it into my side. Stop doubting and believe'" (John 20:26–27). Jesus, once again, showed amazing humility here by condescending to Thomas's request. Jesus lovingly permitted Thomas the skeptic to have the empirical evidence that he had demanded by letting him look at and touch the wounds.

Christ did not want His disciple to remain on the ice in a state of doubt. Instead, He offered Thomas the freedom to investigate His body if that was the proof that he needed to slide toward belief. As far as the record shows, Thomas never took Jesus up on the offer. Instead, he uttered one of the greatest statements of Christ's divinity as he dropped to his knees and said, "My *kyrios* and my *theos*." *Kyrios* is the Greek word for "Lord." *Theos* is the word for "God." The fact that Thomas uttered these words out loud, "Lord and God," and that Jesus and the other disciples did not protest was an amazing statement of faith by Thomas and one of the only places in the Gospels where a disciple directly referred to Jesus as God. Thomas's doubt, whether right or wrong, led him to utter this incredible claim.

It's interesting to note the reasons John included this account in his gospel. In 20:31, John explained that he told the story of Doubting Thomas "that you may believe that Jesus is the Messiah, the Son of God, and that by believing you may have life in his name." It is obvious that John's intention was to help Christians and non-Christians alike deal with doubt. Both skeptics and believers can find common ground with Thomas's desire for visible evidence to answer the questions they have about God.

John also anticipated that controversy would surround the story of the resurrection. Skeptics could argue that if Thomas took the disciples' story at face value, without demanding proof, John's account would lose credibility. The fact is that not all the disciples immediately accepted the news about the risen Jesus. John wisely included the dramatic story of Thomas's slide from doubt to faith to reveal the humanity of the disciple and the authenticity of his return to belief in Christ. Those of us who have not found quick resolution to our own doubt should find hope in this story.

We hear the phrase "It's a journey" quite a bit these days. Most of us can relate to the idea of process, and Thomas's story, like that of John the Baptist's, reveals a man in process in his relationship with God. As a disciple of Jesus, Thomas moved through seasons of great faith as well as those of great questioning. Ultimately, through his apprenticeship, doubt, and bold confession of Jesus as "Lord and God," Thomas stayed faithful in following God to the very end of his life.

Thomas was willing to voice his faith, his questions, and his doubts "out loud" to Jesus and his community. One of the biggest struggles we face is feeling too ashamed to express our doubts to another Christian. It seems Thomas must have battled that same shame. At first, he tried to hide his skepticism by isolating himself, but eventually, he became willing to doubt in community with his fellow disciples. Job moved through this doubt in the same way, and so did John the Baptist. They didn't merely internalize these questions; they talked to someone about them.

The idea that even these close friends of God, these eyewitnesses to His glory, had their doubts comforts me now. Thomas simply did not believe that Jesus was alive, and he just said that out loud. John, facing his death, wondered if Jesus was truly the One. If men who had direct contact with Jesus and saw many miracles performed by His hands doubted, why couldn't I? Why not? Of course it's plausible to doubt God. John doubted. Thomas doubted. Job doubted. I doubted.

I know that I am not in the same league with those guys, but we do share common humanity. Also, Jesus didn't rebuke John the Baptist in his doubts. He did the opposite and encouraged him. He did not condemn Thomas for his doubt in the upper room, either. He admonished Thomas, but not harshly. Perhaps Jesus would not be harsh with me and my doubts. Maybe He wants me to come to Him "just as I am," doubts and all.

Is Seeing Believing?

For a long time, I held on to the idea that if I could just see a miracle, like Thomas or John the Baptist did, then I would believe. But would I really? Fill in the blank with me. *All my doubts would go away if God would* __________. How would you fill in the blank? *If God would only heal my friend of cancer. If God would only bring my child back to church. If God would only make my son stop drinking. If God would only give me some tangible proof of His existence.* We think if God would only honor that one simple request, we would never doubt again. If He would just intervene this once in an undeniable fashion, we feel that we would then be compelled to believe, and all of our doubts would be dispelled.

In the Bible, we see case after case of people witnessing the supernatural power of God and yet still rejecting Him. Pharaoh rejected God after Moses predicted and rained down all the plagues. The Israelites refused to follow God alone after He had parted the Red Sea, provided manna on a daily basis for years, and gave them the Ten Commandments. Many religious leaders who opposed Jesus saw Him heal the sick, cast out demons, and raise a man from the dead, and they still did not believe.

Even people who saw the resurrected Jesus Christ right before their eyes did not believe. Matthew 28:17 says when they saw the resurrected Lord, they worshipped Him, *but some doubted.* Some doubted! Therefore, the idea that we would automatically believe if we could all see a miracle or experience the resurrected Christ is just not so. Sometimes miracles compel people to believe; sometimes they do not.

Jesus spoke to this when he addressed Thomas. "Then Jesus told him, 'Because you have seen me, you have believed; blessed are those who have not seen and yet have believed'" (John 20:29). Jesus granted Thomas's request for more evidence, and Thomas benefited from being able to see the risen Lord right before his eyes. But Jesus was not only speaking to Thomas here. The Lord had the foresight to know that the vast majority of future believers would not have the privilege of seeing Him face to face. He knew we would have to believe without seeing.

Peter wrote to a group of new Christians, in what is now the country of Turkey, to express the same idea of believing without seeing. He said, "Though you have not seen him, you love him; and even though you do not see him now, you believe in him and are filled with an inexpressible and glorious joy" (1 Peter 1:8).

I like that last phrase: "inexpressible and glorious joy." I think everybody desires that joy. And "joy" is the biblical word for deep and meaningful happiness. Everyone wants to be happy, right? But when I look at this verse, a problem arises in my mind. We desire this joy, yet it is tethered to the invisible

Him. It's the same invisible Him that Peter's audience had never seen and never would see, but they believed in Him and loved Him and were filled with this joy.

We're in the same boat. We're never going to see Jesus in our lifetime, but we are urged to believe in Him and trust Him and love Him. Peter says it's this "Him," this invisible One who will give us inexpressible and glorious joy. When I read that, I'm excited on one hand, and I'm confused on the other. And the reason I have questions is that in the last several centuries since the enlightenment, those of us raised in Western culture have been taught this: Seeing is believing. If you see it, you can believe it. If you can't see it, then it's not real. (By the way, if we held consistently to the philosophy that "seeing is believing," then we would lose a lot in this life, things like love, logic, justice, truth, purpose, and hope.) That puts the invisible Him in the "not real" category. But the question remains: If we could see Him, would it really be any easier to believe? Maybe sight, proof, and more evidence is really not what we need at all.

Written in the Stars

Frederick Buechner, in his book *Secrets in the Dark*, gave a creative answer to these cries for objective evidence. The following is my spin on his imaginative story.[6] Imagine if, one dark night, you step outside and look up into the heavens, and somehow the stars in the Milky Way have been reconfigured to spell out these three words: God is Real. (It's written in English of course, because God is an American, right?) You rub your eyes and look again. This can't be real! But there it is, blazing in the sky. God is Real. Of course, you have your cell phone with you because you can't leave home without it. Suddenly calls start flooding in. You're not the only one who sees it! Your brother in the next town is blowing up your phone with texts. Your friends over in England see it too! The neighbors start pouring into the streets, exclaiming, "Look! Look!" Have you seen the stars? Have you seen the Milky Way? Could it be true? "God is Real."

What if that really happened? Some people would just fall down on their knees in fear. Some would be bewildered. "Man, this is wild. There really is a God behind all the universe?" I'm sure some skeptics who've always wondered, "Is there a God?" would find their answer. "Man, there is a God!" What about all the pastors and theologians who secretly kind of always hoped there was a God? They might feel pretty smug. "We were right!" The churches would suddenly be packed with thousands of people, sort of like the reaction after 9/11 when everyone really wanted God to bless America. Maybe some of the older folks would lament, "I can't believe I missed out. There really is a God."

Let's just say that God kept up that light show. Every night, you could go outside, look up into the heavens, and read the proclamation: "God is Real." After a while—let's be honest, we'd need a little bit more, wouldn't we? I mean, wouldn't we want a little more proof, just a little bit more objective evidence?

Perceiving our doubt, perhaps God would start writing in different languages. “God is Real” in Arabic. “God is Real” in Swahili. “God is Real” in Mandarin, Spanish, French. Perhaps every other night, God started writing “God is Real” in a different font. Maybe He would add some celestial music and a laser light show. Perhaps that would convince the rest of the skeptics. “Look—music, colors, lights! God is real—come on! Here is proof!”

Then, as the story goes, perhaps a little boy, ten years old, chewing bubble gum, baseball cap turned backward, walks outside one night. He reads the words lighting up the sky and says, “God is real. So what?”

Perhaps objective proof is really not what’s going to meet the desire, the deep desire of our hearts. Maybe it’s not proof that we’re looking for. Perhaps what we are really longing for is God’s tangible presence in our own lives, and the realization that, just perhaps, He has a plan for us.

But what happens when we feel like His tangible presence can no longer be sensed? Perhaps we can learn from some of the more modern heroes of the faith.

Chapter 5

Famous Doubters

"We were promised sufferings. They were part of the program. We were even told, 'Blessed are they that mourn,' and I accept it. I've got nothing that I hadn't bargained for. Of course it is different when the thing happens to oneself, not to others, and in reality, not imagination."[1]

C. S. Lewis

All my heroes walk with a limp. They limp because their faith was forged in the fires of pain, suffering, and doubt. Dietrich Bonhoeffer, Søren Kierkegaard, and Brennan Manning are all members of the pain club. One was executed by Nazis. Another was ridiculed by society. And the third spent a lifetime battling addiction. I don't get carried away by the latest fad book (unless this volume turns out to be that book), the trendy, tweet-sized philosophy, or the bumper-sticker theological treatise. I just don't have time for that anymore. My Twelve Step friends have an understanding of God that goes far beyond a tweet or a Facebook update. When men and women have suffered greatly, I will eagerly listen to them. Pain cuts through the noise and clutter of modern life. Even before I had personally experienced deep pain in my life, I always seemed to gravitate toward people who had endured pain and hardship and somehow came out on the other side alive. We all must choose who we follow and who we learn from.

I don't understand social media. It baffles me on many levels. I avoided it for over a decade and have just started posting a few quotes online. But I have figured out that one of the goals of social media is to have a lot of followers. I like that term. Everyone is following someone. Throughout my life, I have carefully chosen the people I follow (not on social media, but in real life). I follow men and women who have persevered through the many storms of life and have lived to tell about it.

Throughout my bouts with doubt, I've yearned to find someone to relate to, someone I could follow. Of course I read about Thomas and Job and the father who cried out to Jesus, "I believe, but help my unbelief!" But all of that was in the Bible. What about recent history? Has anyone else wrestled with doubt like I have, or am I all alone?

Over the years, I had read a good amount of church history, but I didn't remember reading about many men and women who had wrestled with doubt. However, as I began to dig further in the quiet history of Christianity, it was there. Deep in the literature found in both the Catholic and Protestant traditions, stories of bouts with doubt were waiting to be told. From Augustine to Martin Luther, from Blaise Pascal to Mother Teresa, many leaders of the church have battled with seasons of intense doubt. Many have walked with a limp.

The Doubts of a Saint

Gallup released a list of the most widely admired people of the twentieth century. The list included Albert Einstein, John F. Kennedy, and Martin Luther King Jr. But topping the list at number one was an Albanian nun, Anjezë Gonxhe Bojaxhiu, known to the world more simply as Mother Teresa.[2]

Well before her canonization as a saint by the Catholic Church in September 2016, Mother Teresa was widely known for her selfless life of service and sacrifice to the sick and dying in the streets of Calcutta, India. Born in 1910 in Skopje, Macedonia, she began her journey as a novitiate in Dublin with the Sisters of Loreto around 1928. She was a high school teacher in Calcutta from 1931–1948, until she helped found the Missionaries of Charity to serve the poorest of the poor with the love of Jesus Christ. Eventually, her amazing work in this horrid city led to worldwide recognition, and she received the Nobel Peace Prize in 1979.[3] When she received the award, Mother Teresa said in her acceptance speech,

> [Jesus] makes Himself the hungry one, the naked one, the homeless one, the sick one, the one in prison, the lonely one, the unwanted one and He says: "You did it to Me." He is hungry for our love, and this is the hunger of our poor people.[4]

We all tend to idolize people. We look up to celebrities, politicians, and business moguls. We imagine that their lives are better than ours or that they breathe rare air. I had the same admiration for such a radical as Mother Teresa. She lived, breathed, and touched death for decades. She poured out her blood, sweat, and tears to comfort the sick and dying in the streets of Calcutta. Her job was brutal and depressing, but she found joy in it. She knew God called her to this horrendous place. I never dreamed a devoted follower of Christ like Mother Teresa could battle enormous doubts. I thought that if you stepped out and did something radical for the faith, then all of your doubts would evaporate. I don't know why I held on to this false belief, but I did. I didn't need to look far to prove that theory wrong. I should have reexamined the many biblical examples of people who did something radical but still had doubts. John the Baptist was radical. He doubted. Thomas was radical. He doubted. David was radical. He doubted. And I found my modern-day example in Mother Teresa.

We identify Mother Teresa as an iconic figure of piety, self-sacrifice, and faith. Most of us didn't know that throughout her life, she felt plagued by the darkness of doubt. She wrote: "I feel just that terrible pain of loss, of God not wanting me, of God not being God, of God not really existing."[5] And in another personal letter, she struggled with accepting the love of Jesus: "Jesus has a very special love for you. As for me, the silence and the emptiness is so great that I look and do not see, listen and do not hear."[6]

Courage to Doubt Out Loud

Mother Teresa's doubt, or dark night of the soul, perplexed her throughout her life. Yet she did not tell any of her close friends about her struggle, with the exception of her spiritual confessors—Archbishop Périer and Father Neuner—who tried to help her get to the bottom of her doubt. They tried to divine what was causing this saintly nun to plunge into seasons of darkness. Périer suggested that it was given to her "like a thorn in the flesh" to prevent her from getting prideful about how successful her mission was in Calcutta. Mother Teresa at first believed Périer's account, that it might be pride or some other sin that was bringing this darkness upon her life.

But it was Neuner who would provide an answer that eventually satisfied this troubled nun.[7] Father Neuner told her, "It was simply the dark night of which all masters of spiritual life know."[8] He counseled her that there was no human remedy or action that she could take to eliminate these seasons, but she needed to see this darkness instead as a type of solidarity with Jesus, "who in His passion had to bear the burden and darkness of the sinful world for our salvation."[9]

Neuner emphasized the hiddenness of God and how Mother Teresa's longing for God's presence actually proved that He was there. Ultimately, it was this dual identification Neuner offered to Mother Teresa that was most helpful. Her bouts with the darkness of doubt could, first of all, allow her to identify with Christ and His feelings of betrayal and rejection. Second, they would allow her to identify more deeply with the rejection, the emptiness, and the pain of the poor in Calcutta whom she was trying to help.[10]

People of faith have been divided over the discovery of Mother Teresa's doubt. Chris Armstrong reported that "the Christian world drew a collective breath of shock when, in 2007, we discovered through a posthumously published book that Mother Teresa of Calcutta had undergone a severe, intense dark night that persisted through almost her entire ministry."[11] When her doubts were publicized around the world, most in the media mocked her, revealing their gross misunderstanding of the nature of faith, doubt, and certainty. They tried to use her doubts against her faith, calling her a hypocrite.

In great contrast, I rejoiced at the revelation and felt a sense of relief. *If it is okay for Mother Teresa to have doubts about God, perhaps it is okay for me.* She was one of the most admired women in the world. She gave her life to serve the poor and dying in one of the biggest slums on the planet. Mother Teresa's doubt helped me, and I believe her doubt can serve as a remedy for us suffering doubters, because the problem for many of us is this—we doubt alone. This loneliness makes us feel that, if we do not have certainty about God or our faith in God, then we are on the verge of losing faith altogether. At best, we feel like second-class Christians.

But doubt is the normal Christian life for many known and unknown saints. Again, the whole idea of faith presupposes doubt. Doubt keeps our faith honest and our prayers real. Doubt gives us some epistemological humility; in other words, we need to accept the truth that no one, I mean no one, can have absolute certainty this side of heaven. Yes, Mother Teresa doubted. She is one of a long line of doubters. It should give us courage to admit our own doubts to ourselves, to others, and especially to God. Once again, there is room for doubt in the life of faith.

Dealing with Doubt: Mother Teresa

In the Catholic tradition, there are mentors called "spiritual directors." Mother Teresa would meet with her spiritual director, Father Neuner, to confess her sins, her problems, and her doubts. She sought wisdom and guidance from this godly counselor. We all need a spiritual director of sorts in our lives. Someone we can go to with all of our pain, fears, and doubts. Life is too complicated to go it alone. Mother Teresa's adviser helped her frame her doubt and gain perspective on it.

Dietrich Bonhoeffer would agree that, when we go through times of uncertainty, we would be helped by receiving words of truth from a trusted friend. Bonhoeffer, who suffered persecution and eventual martyrdom under the Nazis, talks about our need for the Word spoken to us through another person. He writes, "Therefore, the Christian needs another Christian who speaks God's Word to him. He needs him again and again when he becomes uncertain and discouraged, for by himself he cannot help himself by belying the truth."[12]

Bonhoeffer believed that the Word in our friend is stronger than the Word from within. We need someone from the outside to speak the truth to us. When I struggle with doubts, I can go to a friend to confess, question, and cry. Many times, they just listen; at other times, they speak a timely word or offer a simple prayer that brings healing. We can't battle with doubt alone. It just doesn't work.

Again, like Job, Mother Teresa persevered in her relationship with God and was able to doubt out loud to her spiritual director. Her story has the power to infuse courage and faith into fellow doubters who are slipping on the ice. If we look back a little further in church history, we find yet another doubtful heart lurking within one of the most renowned leaders of the Christian faith.

The Doubts of a Leader

One of the most influential figures of the Western world and the leader of the Protestant Reformation was a young monk turned revolutionary named Martin Luther. Born in 1483, Luther transformed the Christian landscape and reluctantly spearheaded a movement that forever changed the map of the Christian faith. Though Luther was best known for his radical faith and individual courage to stand up to the religious hierarchy of his day, he wrestled with doubt throughout his life.

One biographer of Luther, Martin Marty, said, "He makes the most sense as a wrestler with God, indeed, as a God-obsessed seeker of certainty and assurance in a time of social trauma and personal anxiety, beginning with his own."[13]

According to Mark Edwards, "The young Luther's doubt was driven by his fear of death and his doubt that there was a God who can and will raise the dead, but the older Luther's doubts and fears drove him to embrace an epistemology of absolute certainty while lashing out at anyone who would disagree."[14]

Some believe that Luther's doubts were fueled by the parental abuse he suffered as a child. His mother beat him to a point where blood was drawn, and his father frequently flogged him. This has led some scholars to conclude that Luther's harsh view of God as only a God of wrath was a projection of his earthly father onto his heavenly Father.[15]

Luther received a profound sense of peace when he discovered that the righteousness that God demands from people He gives to them in Christ. Yet Luther still struggled with doubt throughout his life. Just a couple of years after the Reformation of 1527, he entered an intense season of doubt and darkness, where he heard a tormenting inner voice that caused him to vacillate on his beliefs. The pressure of possibly leading thousands of people into the fires of hell plunged him into utter despair.[16]

Historian David Steinmetz described the terror that Luther experienced at these times as a fear that "God had turned his back on him once and for all," abandoning him "to suffer the pains of hell." Feeling "alone in the universe," Luther "doubted his own faith, his own mission, and the goodness of God—doubts which, because they verged on blasphemy, drove him deeper and deeper" into despair. His prayers met a "wall of indifferent silence."[17] He experienced heart palpitations, crying spells, and profuse sweating. He was convinced that he would die soon and go straight to hell. "For more than a week I was close to the gates of death and hell. I trembled in all my members. Christ was wholly lost. I was shaken by desperation and blasphemy of God." His faith was as if it had never been. He "despised himself and murmured against God." Indeed, his friend Philip Melanchthon said that the terrors afflicting Luther became so severe that he almost died.[18]

When Certainty Seems Elusive

Anfechtungen was the German word Luther used to describe the spiritual attacks that "kept people from finding certainty in a loving God."[19] Luther experienced many seasons of *anfechtungen*, this almost untranslatable word that he employed, which combined elements of doubt, the dark night of the soul, and the feeling that God has turned His back. Martin Marty wrote:

> Since *Anfechtungen* were rooted in profound doubt, Luther thought that the alluring world and the devil had to be the immediate agents of the taunting. But—and this was much more disturbing—since God was the final determiner of everything, God must either be the stage manager for the drama of doubt or the main actor in causing it. Whenever he reflected on this, Luther said he was left without hope in an abyss of despair.[20]

Looking back at some of my own worst times of doubt, I remember days and months of living in that hopeless abyss. I prayed to God time and time again to bring healing to a loved one who was suffering immense pain. I asked others to pray, I sought wisdom from a vast array of godly counselors, but the situation just got worse. I finally fell in a puddle of tears in our family room and groaned before God. There is nothing quite so troubling and paradoxical as feeling like the One you're crying out to for help is also the One who's allowing the pain to continue. Reflecting back on that moment still unsettles me.

Though Luther frequently wrestled with *anfechtungen*, he saw the benefit to this phenomenon as a means of grace where

God strips you of all certainty and forces you to cling to His Word alone.[21] Though doubt can be harsh and perplexing, it can also be a good teacher and an instigator to lead us into the arms of the Father.

Dealing with Doubt: Martin Luther

Luther dealt with his doubt through a variety of distractions, some healthy and some not so healthy. He was a proponent of listening to music, taking walks, or even drinking to quell his internal struggle. He also warned against trying to process such times alone and emphasized the absolute necessity of voicing doubts out loud to another person. Luther knew our need to hear words of truth from any believer, regardless of their educational background. He said that he would rather have the company of a simple farmworker who believed in God than to be alone to face his doubts.

For me, doubt can be a serious head trip. It's easy to get stuck in my mind, to live only in my thoughts instead of the real world. Some of Luther's tactics for dealing with doubt have helped me. Exercise helps me get out of my head. I know it sounds silly, but to do something physical helps me deal with doubt. I picked up surfing years ago, and I find it very therapeutic. I don't have time to doubt when I'm worrying about drowning or getting eaten by a shark. Sharks and the waves are more pressing issues than the doubts floating through my brain when I am in the ocean. I also surf with friends, which builds a sense of community. I receive great joy from just being in God's creation, watching the sunrise, and catching a wave now and then. In the sea, I feel just how small I am and how powerful God is.

A lot of doubters get stuck indoors and inside their heads. I think it's healthy to get outside and allow God to speak to you through nature. Psalm 19 talks about how the created world constantly communicates the character and nature of God:

> The heavens declare the glory of God;
> the skies proclaim the work of his hands.
> Day after day they pour forth speech;
> night after night they reveal knowledge.
> They have no speech, they use no words;
> no sound is heard from them.
> Yet their voice goes out into all the earth,
> their words to the ends of the world.

Nature is a great teacher. If you doubt, just getting outside every day helps you to get outside your head. Take a walk. Ride a bike. Go for a swim. But I've found a tactic even more elemental.

I have a friend from Mexico who was raised in a dirt-poor, single-parent family. Against the odds, he rose above his circumstances, got a degree, and worked himself into a fortune. But one day, gripped by worry and anxiety, he came home with the weight of the world on his shoulders. As he shared the story of his stress with his wife, their housekeeper overheard and interjected, "Mr. Allen, may I tell you what I do when I feel this way? I get down on my knees and just start to thank God for everything I can think of. And by the time I get off my knees, my worries are gone." I found the simple benefit of this exercise too. When I feel overwhelmed by life, when the problems creep in, when I begin to doubt what God is doing or not doing, I get down on my knees and just start thanking Him. I thank Him for the bed I slept on. I thank Him for my cup of morning coffee. I thank Him that I have a job. I thank Him that I have two legs. I thank Him for all things in life. Staying thankful—and getting specific about it—helps me.

The Doubts of an Intellectual

One of my favorite college courses was a study on C. S. Lewis. No one understood the Christian faith and how to communicate it to the modern world better than Lewis. He possessed an uncanny ability to present a logical, rational case for the Christian faith while simultaneously creating fictional, narrative stories that embodied the essence of the gospel. He was a prolific writer, and his books have influenced both modern and postmodern readers with their vivid imagination and cleverly phrased arguments. The best estimates are that, of his fifty-plus books, more than 200 million copies have been sold,[22] many of his works being turned into movies that have grossed over 1.5 billion dollars around the world.[23] His titles include

The Chronicles of Narnia, The Great Divorce, Mere Christianity, and *Miracles.*

If one had to list the most influential Christians in the past fifty years, C. S. Lewis would certainly be among them. His contributions to the faith rival that of Billy Graham and Mother Teresa. Born in Belfast on November 29, 1898, Lewis was raised in a modest home in Ireland. But when he was nine, his mother died, and he was shipped off to a boarding school in England.

Author Clyde S. Kilby summarized Lewis's journey well in his analysis of *Surprised by Joy*, a brief autobiography of Lewis's younger years:

> It is less an autobiography in an ordinary sense than an account of his religious ups and downs from childhood—of the almost complete lack of religion in his early experience, of his childhood prayer to the Magician God whom he wished to heal his dying mother and then go away, of his first hectic efforts in boarding school to create a satisfying spiritual realization, of his glad retreat into atheism, and then of the long and tortuous return through nature, spiritualism, and philosophy to Theism and finally to Christianity.[24]

One of his tutors at the boarding school was William Kirkpatrick, whom Lewis called "The Great Knock." Kirkpatrick drilled the adolescent Lewis with question upon question that forced him to give reasons and justifications for nearly every word he uttered, eventually turning the young lad into a persuasive debater.[25] This hardened, rationalistic skeptic made a lasting impression on Lewis, but little did The Great Knock realize that he was inadvertently training one of the greatest Christian apologists the Western world would ever know.

As an atheist, Lewis adequately defended his naturalistic view of the universe and came to see Christianity as synonymous with "ugly architecture, ugly music, and bad poetry, and God a great 'Transcendental Interferer.' He wanted to tell God and everybody else that his innermost being was marked 'No Admittance.'"[26] At the same time, Lewis continued to be haunted by this feeling he called "*sehnsucht*." In German, this means "a longing for a deep, lasting joy."

A Slow-Motion Conversion Experience

Through the influence of G. K. Chesterton, Nevill Coghill, George MacDonald, and J. R. R. Tolkien, Lewis slowly and painfully began to doubt his scientific materialism. Gradually, he began to embrace a type of Platonic God, a kind of philosophical absolute he differentiated from "the God of popular religion."[27] As an Oxford professor, he spent much of his alone time in his room in Magdalen, feeling the pursuit of the One he was earnestly trying not to meet.

Then, in the Trinity Term of 1929, Lewis bowed the knee and admitted that "God was God." He described himself that night as "the most dejected and reluctant convert in all England."[28] Lewis explained that this conversion experience "was only to Theism, pure and simple, not to Christianity. I knew nothing yet about the Incarnation."[29]

Sometime later, Lewis traveled to Whipsnade Zoo one sunny morning. About that journey, he said, "When we set out I did not believe that Jesus Christ is the Son of God, and when we reached the zoo I did."[30] From that day forward, he began his journey with God in which he produced more than fifty books, both fiction and nonfiction, several of which gave an intellectual defense of the Christian faith.

Soon after Lewis's life-changing trip to the zoo, he wrote a letter to a friend explaining how, despite the many differences between the denominations and even the big divide between Protestants and Catholics, there existed "an enormous common ground" he called "mere Christianity."[31] In his most well-known apologetic book, *Mere Christianity*, he unpacked the now well-known trilemma concerning the identity of Jesus Christ. Lewis put it plainly that anyone who claimed to be God was either a Liar, a Lunatic, or a Lord,[32] an argument that has persuaded many.

Lewis's slow-motion conversion process involved much doubt and questioning. This was necessary to move him from his atheistic certainty and toward Christianity. Like that of the biblical character Job, Lewis's personal pain and suffering would bring on a season of excruciating doubt and despair.

Crying Out to a Deaf Heaven

It wasn't until later in life that Lewis met and married the love of his life, American writer Joy Davidman. Remarkably, he did so knowing that she was in remission from cancer. He had no false expectations that Joy would live a long life, but when she died four short years after they wed, he was angry and devastated. In the days following her death, Lewis poured out his feelings of grief and doubt in a book called *A Grief Observed.* He had already published a book on pain and suffering entitled *The Problem of Pain*, a rational theodicy, but *A Grief Observed* was raw and personal. Throughout this short book, Lewis cried out in Jobian fashion at a God who seemed silent.

> Meanwhile, where is God? This is one of the most disquieting symptoms. When you are happy, so happy that you have no sense of needing Him, so happy that you are tempted to feel His claims upon you as an interruption, if you remember yourself and turn to Him with gratitude and praise, you will be—or so it feels—welcomed with open arms. But go

> to Him when your need is desperate, when all other help is vain, and what do you find? A door slammed in your face, and a sound of bolting and double bolting on the inside. After that, silence. You may as well turn away. The longer you wait, the more emphatic the silence will become. There are no lights in the windows.[33]

Lewis questioned the goodness of God because He had allowed his precious wife to go through such intense pain. He wrote:

> Not that I am (I think) in much danger of ceasing to believe in God. The real danger is of coming to believe such dreadful things about Him. The conclusion I dread is not "So there's no God after all," but "So this is what God's really like. Deceive yourself no longer."[34]

His complaint is similar to Job's questioning of God's justice and allowance of such senseless pain and agony. As he tossed and turned in his grief, Lewis questioned whether it was rational to believe in a good God or to see Him as "the Cosmic Sadist, the spiteful imbecile."[35] In the midst of his heartache, after the death of his wife, Lewis wondered why this event had caused him to doubt everything concerning his Christian faith.

> Feelings, and feelings, and feelings. Let me try thinking instead. From the rational point of view, what new factor has H.'s death introduced into the problem of the universe?[36] What grounds has it given me for doubting all that I believe? I knew already that these things, and worse, happened daily. I would have said that I had taken them into account. I had been warned—I had warned myself—not to reckon on worldly happiness. We were even promised sufferings. They were part of the programme. We were even told, "Blessed are they that mourn," and I accepted it. I've got nothing that I hadn't bargained for. Of course it is different when the thing happens to oneself, not to others, and in reality, not in imagination.[37]

Lewis was saying, "It's one thing to read about grief; it's another thing to experience it yourself." He was admitting that it is one thing to comfort others in their pain but another thing altogether to be in the pain yourself. After much agony and doubt, Lewis appeared to find some sense of resolve or meaning in Joy's death and the spiritual aftermath that he was experiencing.

He compared his faith in God before the death of his wife to a house of cards, reasoning that nearly everyone's faith in God is in a similar state until they go through some type of suffering or significant trial. He believed the only way to achieve an authentic faith was to see one's house tumble to the ground.

> But of course one must take "sent to try us" the right way. God has not been trying an experiment on my faith or love in order to find out their quality. He knew it already. It was I who didn't. In this trial He makes us occupy the dock, the witness box, and the bench all at once. He always knew that my temple was a house of cards. His only way of making me realize the fact was to knock it down. Getting over it so soon? But the words are ambiguous. To say the patient is getting over it after an operation for appendicitis is one thing; after he's had his leg off it is quite another.[38]

Lewis continued this line of thinking and applied it to both Christians and atheists. He believed that a person never knows whether they are a true Christian or a true atheist unless it becomes a matter of life and death. He even used torture as an analogy to discover the true beliefs of an individual.

> Bridge-players tell me that there must be some money on the game "or else people won't take it seriously." Apparently it's like that. Your bid—for God or no God, for a good God or the Cosmic

> Sadist, for eternal life or nonentity—will not be serious if nothing much is staked on it. And you will never discover how serious it was until the stakes are raised horribly high, until you find that you are playing not for counters or for sixpences but for every penny you have in the world. Nothing less will shake a man—or at any rate a man like me—out of his merely verbal thinking and his merely notional beliefs. He has to be knocked silly before he comes to his senses. Only torture will bring out the truth.[39]

Lewis explained this with a simple but profound analogy:

> The reason for the difference is only too plain. You never know how much you really believe anything until its truth or falsehood becomes a matter of life and death to you. It is easy to say you believe a rope to be strong and sound as long as you are merely using it to cord a box. But suppose you had to hang by that rope over a precipice. Wouldn't you then first discover how much you really trusted it?[40]

C. S. Lewis's conversion story from atheism to theism to Christianity is intriguing, and his honesty is compelling. Listen to what he said: "Now that I am a Christian, I do have moods in which the whole thing looks very improbable, but when I was an atheist, I had moods in which Christianity looked terribly probable."[41]

Lewis maintained a great balance of a heartfelt and intellectually grounded Christian faith. But it doesn't matter how deep or sound your faith in God is. Your world can be rocked by cancer, by death, by suicide. In Lewis's case, like Ted Turner's, it was watching someone he loved slowly die of a disease. The pain of grief cut so deeply that Lewis doubted the goodness, the fairness of God.

When someone of his intellectual and spiritual stature doubts, it gives me hope. I then know I'm not the only one to ask such questions about the character of God. I'm not the only one to doubt the validity of prayer. I'm not the only one who feels like God has abandoned me in the depths of my greatest need. I'm not the only one. Suffering, pain, and death bring you to the edge of faith, doubt, and unbelief. And that's okay. It's interesting that Lewis wrote his "doubt book," *A Grief Observed*, under a pen name. I wonder why? Maybe he, like many of us doubters, felt shame at the raw honesty of his doubts.

Dealing with Doubt: C. S. Lewis

Thankfully, Lewis wrote down his doubts in a journal that became a book. That was one of the ways he dealt with his doubts. I know that he had a close group of friends he met with at the pub on a regular basis and that they also served as a source of encouragement for him. But it is in *A Grief Observed* that we find him venting at God for not healing his wife.

For over a decade, I have seen a gifted therapist on a regular basis. He encouraged me to start journaling my thoughts, my pain, and my doubts years ago, and I have made this a regular part of my life. I don't feel compelled to write in it every day, though during intense times, I do. I just pull up a Word doc and start letting my thoughts flow through the keyboard. My therapist believes there's something healing about externalizing your internal world, getting it out of your head and heart and onto a screen or a piece of paper. That's what Lewis did. If you don't journal, you might think about starting. Write out what happened in your day. Write out your prayers. Write out your doubts. Write out your beliefs. And some days, just write. Don't worry about punctuation and spelling—just let it flow. Be honest. Be brutally honest if you feel like it.

Again, you must dive a little deeper to grasp a more complete picture of C. S. Lewis and these other giants of faith in the history of the church. Lewis, like Job and like Luther, shows that struggle, doubt, and raw grief are all a part of a faith journey with the God who is there and the God who feels like He's not there at times. Madeleine L'Engle summarizes the helpfulness of Lewis's doubt in this way:

> I am grateful, too, to Lewis for having the courage to yell, to doubt, to kick at God with angry violence. This is a part of healthy grief not often

> encouraged. It is helpful indeed that C. S. Lewis, who has been such a successful apologist for Christianity, should have the courage to admit doubt about what he has so superbly proclaimed. It gives us permission to admit our own doubts, our own angers and anguishes, and to know that they are part of the soul's growth.[42]

Mother Teresa doubted. Martin Luther doubted. C. S. Lewis doubted. These are not lightweights. These are the giants of faith worth following. They made their doubt work for them. They integrated doubt into their faith, and their uncertainty about God and the future deepened their faith over time. This makes me feel good.

Perhaps you've spent long enough being hard on yourself for having doubts about God. You may feel like God cannot and will not answer your prayers because of your doubt. I want to give you permission to stop beating yourself up over your doubts. You are normal. It's okay. You are not alone. If God did not want us ever to doubt, He could have reached down and ripped the book of Psalms right out of the Bible.

We can have great doubt and great faith at the same time. Great men and women of faith can also be great men and women of doubt. The two are not mutually exclusive. One of the most painful feelings Lewis dealt with in his doubts was that of disappointment. Where do you go? What do you do when you feel like God has let you down?

Chapter 6

Disappointed with God

"It is difficult to accept that life is difficult; that love is not easy and that doubt and struggle, suffering and failure, are inevitable for each and every one of us."[1]

Michael Leunig

My friend David serves as a lay counselor to thousands of people. I call him the world's best shallow psychologist, but lately he's gotten too deep to maintain that moniker. He's spent countless hours preparing couples for marriage. In his premarital sessions, he frequently lays out the following tough-love truths to the bride-to-be. David says that, somewhere in the first few years, a wife will wake up one day with the following three thoughts:

1. You're not the man I thought you were.
2. You're not meeting my needs.
3. Marriage is difficult.

David is not down on marriage, and he's not just being negative. He's simply trying to adjust a wife's expectations and normalize the feelings most young wives (and some husbands) face when they feel disappointed in their marriage. Most couples go into a marriage with unrealistic expectations of uninterrupted eternal bliss, and when they hit the rugged reality of marriage, they are tempted to bail. Then the doubts creep in. *I wonder why we are having all this conflict. Maybe he's not my soul mate. What if I married the wrong guy?*

I wish David had been in my life years ago to do my pre-theological counseling. He could have coached me about my "personal relationship" with God before I woke up with similar brutal thoughts:

1. You're not the God I thought You were.
2. You're not meeting my needs.
3. Faith is difficult.

I meet people all the time who feel disappointed with God. They read all the wonderful promises in the Bible, then look at their not-so-wonderful lives and start to ask some very searching questions:

What went wrong? I thought God told me I would be married by now, but I'm not. I thought He would protect my family from serious illness, but He hasn't. I simply asked God to keep my marriage together, but He didn't. All I wanted was a better job, and now I am unemployed. I prayed over my children for years, and none of them follow God now. If God really loves me and has a wonderful plan for my life, why did He allow all of this incredible pain and disappointment into my life?

He promised we could move mountains with prayer. He promised that if I trained up my children when they were young, they wouldn't depart from Him. He promised that, if I delighted myself in Him, He would give me the desires of my heart. He promised to never leave me or forsake me. He promised to protect my loved ones from harm's way. He promised. He promised. He said He was a loving Father, but I don't feel loved. Quite the opposite.

In his brilliant book *Reversed Thunder*, Eugene Peterson describes the Christian conundrum of living in the disappointing reality in between the perfection of the beginning in Genesis and the glorious end in Revelation.

> People who live by faith have a particularly acute sense of living "in the middle." … It is routine among us to assume that the beginning was good ("and God saw everything that he had made, and behold it was very good"). It is agreed among us that the conclusion will

> be good ("And I saw a new heaven and a new earth"). That would seem to guarantee that everything between the good beginning and the good ending will also be good. But it doesn't turn out that way … there are disappointments, contradictions, not-to-be-explained absurdities, bewildering paradoxes—each of them a reversal of expectation.[2]

A few years ago, I read a book by Stanley Hauerwas called *God, Medicine, and Suffering*.[3] It tells the stories of children dying of leukemia. Hauerwas juxtaposes these tragic real-life journeys of dying children and their parents with Peter De Vries's novel *The Blood of the Lamb*.[4] The novel tells the story of a struggling first-generation Dutch immigrant, Don Wanderhope, and the horrific loss of his brother, his wife, and nearly his faith. But the coup de grace occurs when his only hope left in this world, Carol, his precious daughter, slowly dies of leukemia.

Carol dies on her fourteenth birthday, a day on which Don was hopeful her doctors were going to provide a drug that would extend her life. When he arrives at the hospital, Carol is dead. Distraught, he leaves and goes to a local bar, then he remembers that he left Carol's birthday cake—white frosting, with Carol's name written in blue—in her room. He travels back up to the room, retrieves the cake, and stumbles into St. Catherine's Catholic Church, a place this former Calvinist frequented during his daughter's illness. In despair, Don screams "No!" to a deaf heaven as he is racked with unbearable pain. He takes the birthday cake and hurls it at the crucifix in the church. Bright blue icing and white frosting drip from the face of Jesus onto the floor.[5] Don Wanderhope feels alone and dead inside. He feels that his God, the One he's hoped in, has devastated his life.

The Winners and the "Others"

If you just read certain parts of the Bible, something we all do, then you set yourself up for disappointment. In other words, we all pick and choose our favorite go-to passages or books in the Bible. They are staples in our spiritual diet that give us a jolt of encouragement, much like a good shot of espresso in the morning. Most of the scriptures we needlepoint and frame, post on Instagram, or print on T-shirts highlight the love of God, the victory we have in following Him, or the abundant life we experience when we surrender to Him.

God does make beautiful, powerful promises in His Word. They are true, real, and good. But here's what makes it difficult and perplexing—some people see multiple promises fulfilled in their lives, and some people just don't. Some of us go through life virtually untouched by tragedy, while others must endure a life of tragedy upon tragedy much like Don Wanderhope's.

Earlier we looked at Hebrews 11, which contains a list of men and women who entered the "Hall of Fame of Faith." The chapter talks about how Abraham offered his only son as a sacrifice, how Moses rescued his people from slavery, and how Rahab the prostitute took the risk and hid the spies in her home. In verses 33–35a, the writer vamps about how other people by faith conquered kingdoms, administered justice, shut the mouth of lions, quenched the fury of flames, routed foreign enemies, and even received people back from the dead. When I read that passage, I am exuberant with praise and filled with great expectations. But then, the author of Hebrews takes a sharp turn with three simple words: "There were others."

That's how verse 35b lets the air out of the hyper-faith balloon. There were others … There were others who were tortured, flogged, imprisoned, stoned to death, sawed in two, and decapitated by the sword. There were others who were destitute, persecuted, and mistreated. There were others who wandered in deserts and mountains and lived in caves and in holes in the ground. The "others" were commended for their faith but did not receive what was promised. Brutal.

I met some friends of mine at Carrabba's for lunch recently. We enjoyed some wonderful Italian food and caught one another up on our lives. One of the gentlemen at the table is the pastor of a church that could be called "*There Were Others* Community Church." For my friend's safety, I won't mention the location of his church, but suffice it to say it is situated in one of the most violent places on planet earth. The amount of suffering, pain, torture, death, and persecution his members have endured is incalculable. Mind boggling. Tragic. Horrific. At the same time, the church is growing, and hundreds are coming to know

Christ. They are a part of this Hebrews 11:35b "Hall of Fame of Faith." They have to live out their faith each day knowing it could be their last. For them, suffering and persecution is the normal Christian life.

I realize that this seems like an extreme example. To some of our privileged ears, it is. But there have been millions of Christians who have gone through this same kind of suffering. We may experience other degrees of relentless pain when we deal with a chronic illness, a child who's addicted to drugs, or a family member who requires twenty-four-hour medical care each and every day. "There were others …" helps give perspective to the brutal elements that hit some of us in this life. Some endure a tough season of pain, while others must endure and learn to find God in an entire lifetime of pain. If you are one of the "others," it does not mean that God has left you. God loves you. God cares for you. God is with you as you walk through this life.

We'd all like to be included in the blessed life of Hebrews 11:1–35a, wouldn't we? None of us would choose to live south of verse 35a, but that's where many of us find ourselves.

Reading verse 35b and the tragic stories that follow used to trouble me, but it doesn't anymore. As a matter of fact, I find great comfort in these excruciatingly tough words. In a way, these verses normalize much of the pain, suffering, and mind-blowing heartache many of us must endure in this life. Life on the dark side of verse 35 hurts, but it helps to know we're not alone in this. God has not forgotten or forsaken us. The men and women who are on the B side are just as precious in God's sight as the men and women on the A side.

I have a question I like to ask people: "If you were going to be alone on a desert island for fifteen years and could bring only five books of the entire Bible, which books would you bring?"

Of course, there are no right or wrong answers, but the five I pick are:

1. Genesis
2. John
3. Romans
4. Hebrews
5. Psalms

I put Psalms at number five on my list, but that's not because it's the least important. The Psalms express the language of the heart. The Psalms teach us how to pray, how to praise, and how to pound heaven with the raw emotions of our souls. Some psalms lift our spirits so high we feel like heaven has come to earth, while other psalms take us so low we wonder if the guy who wrote them was even a believer. The Psalms beckon us to sing, shout, and celebrate. The Psalms allow us to cry, question, and doubt. I guess another way to say it is the Psalms give us the freedom to be human. Human beings striving to process life on earth as it unfolds one day at a time. Life with all its beauty, all its pain, and all its color.

Some psalms seem to flow from a heart with little to no faith whatsoever. They're a running rant against God for not answering prayer. In Psalm 88, the writer relentlessly pours out his pain and disappointment at God. He hurls every birthday cake he can find into the invisible face of God. He feels like God has abandoned him and thrown him into a bottomless pit. He cries to God, "I'm battered by your rage and relentless pounding on me. You have turned my friends against me. You are turning a deaf ear to me. You haven't shown up. I'm black, blue, and bloodied. You've beaten me up so badly that I am about to die here. My lover and my neighbor dumped me. Darkness is my only friend."

And that's how Psalm 88 ends, with those five frightening words: "Darkness is my only friend" (HCSB). But that's real life. That's real pain. That's real disappointment. Thankfully, most of the Psalms seek out some form of resolution to the pain and darkness.

The Language of Faith and Doubt

"My God, my God, why have you forsaken me?" Most people can attribute this phrase to Christ in the Gospels.[6] True. On the cross, Jesus repeated this cry as He hung suspended between heaven and earth. But this phrase was first found on the lips of David in the Old Testament. David penned these words in Psalm 22 centuries before the crucifixion. In this psalm, he lays out a pattern of how he worked out his faith in the midst of doubt.

Look at the pattern of wavering doubt and faith found in just this one psalm. He starts off with *doubt*: My God, my God, why have You forsaken me? Why are You waiting so long to rescue me? I am crying out to You in anguish every day, but You don't answer. I can't sleep at night; it's killing me.

Then he transitions in the next few verses to *faith*: Yet You are the one God. My ancestors trusted in You and You did not let them down. They cried out to You and You delivered them.

Then he switches back to *doubt*: But I am a worm. People insult me and mock me for trusting in You, Lord. They hurl insults at me.

And in the next verses, back to *faith*: Yet You brought me into this world and made me trust in You. You have been my God since birth. Be close to me, God, for I'm in trouble. Help me.

And then he's back to *doubt*, describing how he feels: I feel surrounded by a bunch of bulls. Roaring lions open their mouths to devour me. I'm melting on the inside like wax, and all of my bones are out of joint. My mouth is so dry my tongue sticks to the roof of my mouth. Mad dogs surround me, and my hands and feet are pierced. I'm emaciated to the point that others see my bones protruding through my skin.

Then he circles back to *faith*: Be near to me, God. Help me. You are my strength. My life is precious to me; save me. And he then goes on to say what he will do when God comes through. He will praise God in the assembly. And eventually God is going to make all things right and beautiful that we might live with Him forever and ever.

Notice how David swings back and forth, from doubt to faith, and from faith to doubt. It's like he can't decide. He's in the middle. He's sliding on the ice. Eventually, he lands back on solid ground with God as he awaits the outcome of his cry for help. Emily Dickinson says it well: "We both believe and disbelieve a hundred times in an hour, which keeps believing nimble."[7]

I remember days of being tossed back and forth between doubt and faith. Almost every day, I would wake up early in the morning, go into my closet, and start the day strong with a great time of prayer and Bible study. But only hours later, I would waver. Did God really hear my prayers? Is He really there? Later on the same day, and for no particular reason, I would return to a position of faith and trust. I felt like a spiritual schizophrenic, caught in a doom loop of questioning, crying, and trusting. Though I anguished and toiled in this spiritual spiral, I failed to voice these emotions out loud to God. Nor did I talk to friends about my deep disappointment with God. I didn't know how to reconcile the presence of doubt alongside the path of faith.

When I look back at my inaugural season of doubt, I think, *What an idiot.* My doubts all started when I felt as though God had let me down. I attempted to be radical for God by believing He would do radical things for me and my friends. But when He didn't do anything, I felt left in the lurch. I thought prayer didn't work, and perhaps God didn't work. I wasn't asking much—not as much as David in his life-or-death crisis, not as much as parents begging for the life of their dying child. I just wanted more of God. I wanted a bigger God. *I will believe in You if You do a miracle. Perform for me, God.* I wanted proof. I wanted strong faith, miracle faith. I wanted to be sold out for God because He showed up and put on a show. That would impress me. That's what I wanted as a kid.

I'm past that now. Don't get me wrong. I would be elated if God did heal someone I knew who was suffering or if He performed an amazing miracle before my eyes. I'd welcome it, but I don't seek it. I want to know God, to love God, and to let God love others through me. If He provides some supernatural signs and wonders along the way, that's wonderful, but it's not the main thing.

Sure, I am thrilled when I hear happy-ending stories that can only be explained by God Himself intervening. But I am more impressed with the Dietrich Bonhoeffers, Joni Eareckson Tadas, and Jerry Sittsers of the world. Men and women who have persevered in their faith. Men and women who have faced devastating disappointment in their own lives and come out on the other side still loving and trusting God. Men and women of deep faith, deep character, and deep humility. That's what impresses me. Those faithful friends who have lived south of verse 35a for a long time.

Here's an interesting fact: all the people Jesus healed still eventually died. The healing was just a bandage to stave off the inevitable. Even Lazarus had a second funeral that finally took. I want to be clear here: I love miracles. I believe in miracles. I pray for miracles. But my faith is not based on how God answers my prayers. I choose to live in the tension of *not my will, but Thy will be done*. Some days, I just trust God and let the chips fall where they may. And other days, I feel like Don Wanderhope, contemplating why I feel so let down by my God who loves me deeply but allows such pain and disappointment to come my way.

After Don throws the cake at the crucifix, Stanley Hauerwas comments on this excruciating scene:

> So Wanderhope's anguished "No!" was perhaps his most determinative act of faith. In that "No" he joined that great host of the faithful who believed that the God they worshiped is not a God who needs protection from our cries of pain and suffering. Ironically, the act of unbelief turns out to be committed by those who refuse to address God in their pain, thinking that God just might not be up to such a confrontation.[8]

For years, I refused to address God in my pain, doubt, and disappointment. I just suppressed it or tried to hide it from God and others. I allowed the doubt and disappointment to dwell inside my head, and that produced a lot of anxiety, fear, and shame. It was like allowing a form of mental cancer to rent space in my mind.

Can God Handle Your Pain and Doubt?

The proper treatment here is to pour it all out before God, a trusted friend, or a therapist. God can handle your pain, frustration, and doubt. Like Job, like Thomas, like Don, the best cure is to doubt out loud. Pour out your raw emotions to the One who knows you and loves you right where you are. And perhaps when you wake up once more with those three tough realities …

1. You're not the God I thought You were.
2. You're not meeting my needs.
3. Faith is difficult.

… you will realize that it's all a part of having an authentic relationship with God and those doubts can actually be strengthening your faith. Disappointment produces doubts that can lead to a stronger faith—if you're willing to lean in to your doubts.

Chapter 7

Searching for Certainty

"Doubt is not a pleasant condition, but certainty is absurd."

Voltaire

Nothing tears a country apart like a civil war. Families fight against families; friends turn into enemy combatants—it's a brutal battle where long-term alliances are split in two. When you are in the middle of a bout with doubt, it can feel like an internal war. A part of you wants to hold on to these cherished beliefs, but another part of you seems to be waging war against these beliefs.

When I was trying to fight my way out of my long battle with doubt, it felt like a civil war was raging inside my head.

I was an internal agnostic and an external Christian. I remember being the speaker at a weekend discipleship camp for high school students, spending hours and hours teaching these guys the basics of Christianity and challenging them to take their faith to the next level. But before I led the sessions, waves of doubt hit me again and again. I prayed. I cried. I asked God to remove the doubts, but they kept coming. I had to peel myself off the floor and pull myself together in order to go out and teach the next sessions. I hated feeling like a fraud. I was a divided man.

I led other youth retreats, taught Bible studies, prayed daily, and still attended church on Sundays and hoped to see God's supernatural intervention in my life. I felt like such a hypocrite and a fake, but I somehow knew that God was alive and real for other people. That's what was crazy about all of my doubts. A part of me wanted desperately to believe in the God and Jesus of my youth; another part of me thought the whole thing seemed preposterous. I was split. Torn in two. My brain and heart had taken up arms against each other.

Psychologists have a term for this mental war: cognitive dissonance. Cognitive dissonance describes the discomfort that most of us feel when we encounter information that contradicts our existing set of beliefs or values. An uneasiness creeps in when we attempt to hold two contradictory thoughts or ideas at the same time, and this state of mind makes us feel divided and incongruent.

Leanne Payne frames it like this—we have a rational side of our mind and an intuitive side of our mind. They work together and provide balance and stability. But when we enter a season of extreme doubt, it's like the rational side of our mind eats up the intuitive side of our mind.[1]

Forgetfulness is one of the traps we fall into when the rational side of our mind is devouring the intuitive side. We forget our Ebenezers—those moments in life when God intervened or when we sensed His presence in an unusual way. Hyper-rationalizing clouds our memories of God's powerful presence in our lives. We must refuse to doubt in the dark what we have believed in the light.

My cognitive dissonance, this inner turmoil, created a sense of insecurity. I felt I had lost my foundation and wanted desperately to get it back. I have met so many people who have felt the same way, fellow doubters who said, "I've got to find certainty again." Most of them, including myself, searched diligently to regain some semblance of security. We will see later in this chapter where that search led us, but for now let's uncover why this search for certainty was so vital. Where in the world did this desire for certainty come from?

When you are sliding on the ice of doubt, it is helpful to know where that doubt comes from. Why do we ask questions about reality that other cultures don't? When I get sick, I want to know what I have and how I got it. When we go into a time of doubt, it is helpful to know what kind of doubt we have and how we got it. Understanding something of the origin of doubt can help diagnose the type of doubt we may be experiencing.

Our Modern Worldview

First, it is beneficial for us to have a grasp of the philosophical soil that has allowed doubt to flourish in the Western world. Every society maintains certain norms, habits, and values that are assumed. Those assumptions are the beliefs that make up our worldview. Most of us are too busy just trying to survive and put bread on the table to consciously analyze such matters. As Westerners, the cornerstone of our worldview is to question and doubt. For centuries, we have favored the mind and the sciences as reliable ways of knowing what is actually real. You can look at the following section as a type of insider's guide that explains why we live in a culture that embraces so much doubt and continues to search for that elusive certainty.

A Brief History of Doubt

In premodern times, the Western world enjoyed a sense of certainty they gleaned from the church and its crude interpretation of the cosmos. When Galileo pulled out his telescope and proved that the earth orbited around the sun, not the other way around, the worldview of the entire culture sank into uncertainty. No longer could people trust what they could see with the naked eye. If they had been deceived by something as "clear" as the sun orbiting the earth, what else had fooled them? This created enormous insecurity and fear that the church leaders had let them down as well. The church decided to mobilize some brilliant scientists and philosophers to rebuild an edifice of certainty.

Modernism is a term used to describe this search. This cultural movement can be traced back to the Enlightenment period, which began in late seventeenth-century Europe. Modernism stressed the ideas of reason, logic, and the scientific method as primary ways of knowing, as opposed to tradition and the authority of the church.[2] Though many of this movement's leaders were Christians, or at least claimed to be Christians, their new ways of knowing eventually provided the foundations for skepticism toward the Christian faith and even for outright atheism.

While expressing doubts toward religious belief, modernism's advocates believed that they could arrive at certainty about the nature of the universe through logic, reason, and scientific experimentation. It was by these navigational devices that people could sail confidently through the waters of reality, completely apart from any revelation of God. Pierre-Simon Laplace typified modernism's sentiments after he gave Napoléon an account of the history of the cosmos. When asked by Napoléon why he had made no mention of God in his account, Laplace quipped, "Sir, I have no need of that hypothesis."[3]

Descartes's Doubting Experiment

One of the most influential leaders in modernism has to be René Descartes (pronounced Day-cart), who lived from 1596 to 1650. Descartes, who was commissioned by the church, sought to establish a body of knowledge that was certain in order to rescue the people of his time from the doubt created by Galileo's invention of the telescope.[4] He garnered the title "the father of modern philosophy" because of his unique faith in the ability of the human mind to solve all problems of the universe and thus build a structure of knowledge that was indubitable.[5] I realize this is heady stuff, but stay with me here.

Descartes, and his method of systematic doubt, attempted to reestablish certainty—not in the senses, but in the mind. His method started with a distrust in knowledge passed down by those in authority coupled with a distrust in knowledge received through the senses. In order to build this edifice of certain knowledge, Descartes began by asking the simple question, "Am I absolutely certain this is true?"[6] He believed that by asking such questions that arise from doubt, you could eventually push past the untrustworthy knowledge derived from authority and sensation and delve into what was unquestionably true.

Descartes's doubt operated on three levels:

> **Level one: Doubt the senses** because they are an unstable source of knowledge. Descartes used the classic example of a stick in water that

appears crooked. One's sight tells you the stick is bent, but in reality, it is straight.

Level two: Doubt propositions that you might have thought were impervious to doubt. The computer screen in front of you may seem obvious, but Descartes would say that you could be dreaming and, in reality, be at home asleep in your bed.

Level three: Doubt all sensory information because it might be created by a malignant demon that has deceived the mind. Like the movie *The Matrix*, Descartes theorized that there may be no external world at all; it may just be a demonic illusion on a grand scale.[7]

After doubting everything known and available to him, Descartes finally arrived at a foundation that he perceived could not be shaken: *cogito, ergo sum*, which means "I am thinking, therefore I am." No matter how strongly and thoroughly he pushed doubt to its limits, he could not doubt that he was a thinking being. Even if he doubted, he was still thinking, which in turn proved his existence. From this simple foundation, Descartes began to build his structure of certainty.[8]

Descartes simply gave human reason too much credit. I respect his Herculean attempt to ground certainty in the mind; however, he failed to realize that reason alone was not up to the task. Reason is great. Reason is wonderful. Reason can take you a long way. But reason is limited. Reason is tainted. Reason is biased. God never intended for us to figure it all out on our own. He did not design us to make sense of life by merely using our reasoning capabilities. He designed us for faith. For trust. Of course we reason, we think, but we also know by trusting. By living out what He has called us to do. Human reason should recognize its limits and believe that it can learn from a Being with superior powers. Admit that our reason is powerless to figure out this world and our lives, and turn ourselves over to the Power who gave us the ability to reason in the first place.

Faith requires beliefs that are above reason. That's how God set it all up. It's healthy and life giving to come to that conclusion. It's arrogant to give our minds and our reasoning powers too much credit. But at the same time, we have to realize that once we've engaged our minds, there is yet another gear, and that gear is faith.

Decades later, David Hume refuted Descartes's rationalism in favor of a new brand of empiricism, one that attempted to find certainty in the senses, not the mind. But as Hume pushed his own empiricism to its limits, he arrived at the conclusion that there is no certainty to be had and that "the only alternative seemed to be a refusal to commit oneself to any one spot for very long for fear of sinking without a trace."[9]

Hume was followed by Immanuel Kant, who attempted to synthesize Descartes's rationalism with Hume's empiricism. And when Kant implied that "ultimate reality is unknowable" (i.e.,

God cannot be known), this statement would become indelibly etched in the soul of the Western mind and plunge the modern world deeper into this "culture of doubt."[10] I need to restate the fact that both Descartes and Kant were Christians, but their exclusive ways of knowing and doubting paved the way for skepticism and for the rise of atheists to permeate our culture.

Our Postmodern Worldview

Postmodernism is the intellectual movement that tore a gash in the underside of modernism, causing it and all its certainty to sink. Ironically, postmodernism sprang from modernism, since skepticism undergirds both. I heard a lecture by scholar Peter Enns, who put it this way:

> It has been said that postmodernism is simply modernism taken to the next step: it's being skeptical about modernist skepticism. So, modernism celebrates the triumph of western rationalist positivistic Enlightenment ways of knowing, and postmodernism says that there are different ways of knowing that aren't western but just as legitimate.[11]

Modernism was the unsinkable ship of certainty produced by the twin forces of rationalism and empiricism. But ironically, the skepticism behind both of these forces proved to be modernism's undoing. Skeptics simply followed the logical next step of questioning the legitimacy of rationalism and empiricism. Thus, in postmodern thinking, the skepticism unleashed by modernism turns on itself and deconstructs all previous forms of knowing.

A related key component of postmodernism is perspectivalism, which you can view as a type of doubt. This philosophy means that every theory, every idea, every person, and every people group approaches life from a particular perspective or worldview. These worldview assumptions represent a bias that cannot be ignored when evaluating research or history.

Thus, for example, one's interpretation of a historical event is controlled by his or her perspective. A military event was a glorious victory if seen from the perspective of the winner. But it was an unspeakable tragedy if seen from the perspective of the loser. Since a common postmodern sentiment is that "history is always written by the winners," perspectivalism would dictate that the official record of the historical event be examined with suspicion, that is, doubt. It is only a perspective and not fact. Perspectivalism would further seek to counteract the potential oppression of winners imposing their power on losers by giving a voice to the oppressed and marginalized people throughout history and in the world today.[12]

Perspectivalism can lead to either healthy doubt or unhealthy doubt. On the unhealthy side, it could cause you to doubt whether the objective truth claims in the Bible are valid since the authors are culturally and religiously biased. Perspectivalism could lead to a perpetual state of doubt about any truth claims, given the reality that every human views history, experience, and reality itself through his or her own set of lenses.

On the healthy side, it could give you a sense of humility when presenting the truth claims of Scripture. To ignore the context, various translations, and variances in the Bible and act as if all the authors are writing from an objective perspective is not only naïve; it negates the human element of divine inspiration. If there is a God and if He has revealed Himself through a book and through a person, He can speak objective truths through subjective individuals.

Fundamentalism Sells Certainty

I feel that acknowledging the various perspectives of the authors and how that played into their writing of Scripture is realistic and healthy. For so long, we assumed the same starting point for knowledge as any modernist would: claim that there is objective truth and that it can be found using human reasoning and senses. This assumption was both implicit and explicit, depending on whom you read. At the same time, the go-to intellectual tactic for most Christians has been to challenge seekers and even believers to just "examine the facts" of the Christian faith. This challenge gets made as if the facts of the Christian faith can be examined in the same way one would conduct a science experiment. Perspectivalism ushered in some healthy doubt to counter this modern but failed way of knowing.

In other words, a Christianity made up entirely of certainty is just a modernized version of Christianity. Most fundamentalists sell certainty. Fundamentalist Christians sell certainty and ground their certainty in the Bible. Fundamentalist Muslims sell certainty and ground their certainty in the Koran. Fundamentalist atheists sell certainty and ground their certainty in science. Fundamentalist agnostics sell certainty and ground their certainty in perpetual doubt. So the bottom line is that certainty sells.

No one wants to live in uncertainty. No one wants to have this cognitive dissonance, this civil war raging inside their mind. That's the appeal of any type of fundamentalism. Be it theistic or atheistic, fundamentalism offers rational certainty. It quells the demon of cognitive dissonance by giving you an assurance about how this world truly works and villainizes anyone who dissents from this view. I think Robertson Davies said it best: "Fanaticism is … overcompensation for doubt."[13]

Lesslie Newbigin, the famous missions theorist, criticized parts of the Christian church for attempting to match Enlightenment certainty with its own brand of Christian certainty.[14] Both atheistic and Christian modernists believed they had obtained objective truth that was unquestionable, that could give one a sense of certainty. But this kind of certainty can have disastrous effects.

Take former Christians, like Bart Ehrman, as I mentioned previously, who left the fold because they did not find the rational certainty they were promised by their evangelical pastors and professors.[15] But also consider other Christian thinkers, such as Gregory Boyd and Daniel Taylor, who discovered a more resilient faith.[16] They found the search for certainty empty and were able to incorporate their uncertainty and doubt into a robust faith. I feel the same way. Certainty seems ultimately elusive.

Within the Western world at large, modernism gave secularists who wanted a sense of certainty a savior, a certainty that can be gained through both reason and the scientific method. Modernists seized this certainty and did a very effective job of marginalizing Christian beliefs by presenting the scientific method as the only legitimate form of knowledge and mocking Christian truth claims as myths and fairy tales. This led some Christians to a type of doubt that led to unbelief.

When I talk with Christians and non-Christians, I still find that many hold on to the belief that a group of scientists, in some secret laboratory, wearing long white coats and goggles, have a corner on certainty that no one else possesses. Some Christians fear this reality to be true and want to run from science, or at least demonize it. Because some renowned scientists loudly mock the Christian faith, some groups of believers feel that science itself is antagonistic to Christianity.

I'm thankful to know many devoted Christians like Jim Tour and John Lennox, Christians who are also influential scientists. Their faith in God informs and enlightens their scientific endeavors, while skeptics continue to rely on the authority of the secular expert they "know" exists somewhere. The truth is, those chemists, physicists, and biologists who work in the hard sciences "know" that this Holy Grail of knowledge doesn't exist, but still the myth of scientific certainty looms large in our culture.[17]

The postmodernists came on the scene and revealed the biases of the so-called detached, objective observer. They showed how scientists and rationalistic philosophers were just as biased as any religious believer. Postmodernism appears to discourage any attempt at finding truth, external or internal, and instead preaches a gospel of perpetual doubting. In this way, both modernists and postmodernists utilized doubt in different ways to undermine some basic tenets of the Christian faith. Postmodernism led to this type of deification of Doubt. Dallas Willard summed up that sentiment well: "We live in a culture that has, for centuries now, cultivated the idea that the skeptical person is always smarter than the one who believes. You can almost be as stupid as a cabbage as long as you doubt."[18]

If you are still awake or your brain is not completely scrambled, I hope you can see why this chapter means a lot to me and for those who struggle with doubt. Doubt is not only in our human DNA; it's also deeply ingrained in the DNA of our culture. We believed that the mind could give us certainty, but it did not. We believed the sciences could give us certainty, but they did not. We believed religion could give us certainty, but it did not. I finally decided that I should let go of certainty. But how on earth do you do that?

Chapter 8

Letting Go of Certainty

"Faith is embracing the uncertainties of life. . . .
It is recognizing a divine appointment when you see one.
Embrace relational uncertainty. It's called romance.
Embrace spiritual uncertainty. It's called mystery. . . .
Embrace occupational uncertainty. It's called destiny.
Embrace intellectual uncertainty. It's called revelation."[1]

Mark Batterson

Over the years, people came from all over the world to seek the wisdom of Mother Teresa. One of those seekers was a philosopher and professor named John Kavanaugh. Kavanaugh traveled thousands of miles to Calcutta to meet with this revered spiritual leader in hope of receiving some guidance. On his first morning there, Mother Teresa asked Kavanaugh why he had journeyed such a long distance to visit her in the "house of the dying."

Kavanaugh replied, "I want you to pray for me."

She asked, "How can I pray for you?"

He said, "Pray that I have clarity."

Mother Teresa responded, "That I will not do." Her response stunned Kavanaugh, so he asked her why she would not pray for him to have clarity.

She smiled and said, "Clarity is the last thing you are clinging to and must let go of."[2]

I like this simple story. Clarity, like certainty, can become an idol. Kavanaugh, like most of us, wanted certainty that his next steps were the right ones … the steps God wanted him to take. Mother Teresa knew such certainty was not available, so she chose to tell him that he must let go of that desire.

We all cling to someone or something. Kavanaugh wanted certainty about God's will for his life. I wanted certainty about the nature and workings of God. I clung to certainty for a long time—about two decades, in fact.

Losing My Religion

I once believed I had certainty because what was given to me was truth. The Bible was true. Jesus was true. He told me how to live here and now and how to go to heaven when I die. We were right, and everyone else was wrong. There are Christians and non-Christians. Those who believe the truth and those who don't believe the truth. I prayed. I believed. I had a childlike faith.

Not only did I believe, but I lived out my faith as well. I didn't drink or party. I read the Bible every day. I prayed every day. I taught Bible classes from the time I was fifteen years old. I went street witnessing. I fasted and prayed. I had zero doubt about God, Jesus, the Bible, and my relationship with Him. Absolute confidence, 100 percent certainty. I relished that season of my life. I have good friends, godly friends, analytical friends who still have that degree of certainty and have never wavered. I look at that kind of certainty as a gift from God.

During that season of certainty, I felt like I checked all the right boxes. I had my morning quiet time. Check. I evangelized lost people and even went door to door like a Jehovah's Witness. Check. I attended church and Sunday school. Check. I tithed. Check. I served in the church. Check. Then there was the list of activities I refrained from. I did not party. I did not drink. I did not go to movies. I did not listen to secular music. At that time, I felt like I did all the right things and refrained from doing all the wrong things. I saw myself as a committed Christian.

Looking back on that season now, though, I can see that I was misguided. Many of the spiritual disciplines I practiced were good, and avoiding those "worldly" activities didn't hurt anything, but I missed what Jesus was really all about—grace. I had no clue about the grace of God and how to share that with others. I was caught up in my little world of religious rules—things I did and didn't do. I did not take the time to serve, to love, and to meet people where they were. I was a modified Pharisee but didn't even know it. My certainty was grounded in my Christian morality and my sense that we were right and others were wrong.

I felt like God desired absolute certainty from me. I had to be absolutely sure that if I died right now I would go to heaven because I had earnestly prayed the "sinner's prayer." As many preachers put it back then—and you've heard me quote this before, so say it with me: "You've got to know that you know that you know." Also, I believed I had to be absolutely certain when I went to God with a prayer request in order for Him to answer it in the affirmative. Didn't the Bible say you must be sure when you go to God in prayer? Didn't Jesus rebuke His followers for doubting and being men of "little faith"? I believed those words. I was ready to step out of the boat and watch God perform miracles.

If I believed the Bible was inerrant and its supernatural accounts were real, then why not try some of that myself? I thought visible proof of God's power in my life would help people come to know Christ. I thought it was the next logical step in my life of faith. It would be like taking the training wheels off a bicycle or free-climbing a mountain face without safety ropes. But when I tried to walk on water, when I prayed for miracles and the miracles didn't happen, I sank. Down, down, down to the bottom of the sea.

I panicked, as Peter did, but there was no literal Jesus to pull me up. I started praying for big things like healings and raising people from the dead. I prayed with certainty, and still nothing happened. *Why doesn't God answer my prayers? I'm praying in His will. I'm not praying for a Porsche or even a pay raise. I just want to see this person healed.* When the miracles failed to materialize, I was sucked into a whirlpool of questions and confusion.

At the time, I hated being in this perpetual state of doubt. When you stay there for very long, despair creeps in, and that's a painful place to be. I needed some serious help to escape from this quagmire. So I studied the intellectual foundations of Christianity and amassed a large library of works from brilliant thinkers who gave me great answers to some of my questions but not the certainty I longed for. I studied different methods that Christians utilized over the years to defend against the questions of skeptics—the classical approach, the evidential approach, the presuppositional approach, and the existential approach. I listened to debates between atheists and Christians to buttress my faith and quiet my uncertainty. I passionately pursued this path in an attempt to regain the certainty I had lost. But still I circled the drain of doubt.

Searching for Certainty in the Greek

One of the misguided ways I was taught to find certainty was by having the "right" translation of the Bible. The New American

Standard version was the coin of the realm at that time. Most conservative pastors preached from the NASB because they felt it got you closer to the original Greek; therefore, you had more certainty and accuracy about what the various writers of Scripture were saying. I remember, when I was brimming with certainty, I used to mock people for reading or preaching from the New International Version or other translations besides the NASB. I thought I was pretty funny, saying, "You're using a watered-down version of the Bible. I hope you don't get wet carrying that thing around with you." I had my devotions from the NASB, and I taught from the NASB. After all, it was the most literal translation you could find.

Some people fall into doubt during seminary. I got a head start and was well into my bout with doubt before I even arrived. I hoped the information and knowledge I would gain at seminary would bring back the certainty I had lost. I reasoned that if the NASB gave me a degree of certainty, knowing the original Greek would give me even more certainty.

If Paul, John, Luke, and others wrote scripture in the Greek language, and if I could master this language, perhaps I could master knowing God. That was my mind-set. If the NASB was the most literal translation, then why stop there? Why not pursue it further and learn the original language of the New Testament? Then I could know with absolute certainty what Scripture said. I thought an English translation was secondhand at best, and I reasoned that the Greek could be the key to unlocking the certainty code in my life.

I studied Greek under a godly professor named Tommy Lea. And, by the way, I discovered that the NASB was a darn good translation of the Greek. I remember sitting in class one day and listening to Dr. Lea lecture. He was discussing the Scripture and the Greek text, and then he began to say something like, "Well, that's only one interpretation of this passage in the Greek; there is another interpretation by other scholars and yet another interpretation by this scholar." It was like my hope had been dashed on the rocks. If top-flight scholars couldn't agree and have certainty about the Greek, how could a peon like me achieve it? No one seemed to have it. I was crushed. For the record, I still believe knowing Greek is helpful, but it's not a guarantee of finding certainty.

I never found the slam-dunk piece of evidence or iron-clad argument that would prove the objective truthfulness of Christianity once and for all. Oh, how I craved this sense of rational and emotional certainty! I reached for it with all my might but never grasped the handle. I never found that certainty. Not in Christianity, not in reason, not in science. Gradually, God used several "mentors" in my life to guide me in a direction away from that frustrating, elusive search. I use the term "mentors" loosely, and soon you'll know why.

My Mentor in Doubt

Daniel Taylor, whom I referred to in chapter 2, was one such mentor. I stumbled upon a book he wrote called *The Myth of*

Certainty, and through his writings, this wise man helped me start the slow process of letting go of the search for certainty. Taylor simultaneously dismantled the faux certainty of science and the Christian version of it. When it comes to attaining knowledge about nonphysical things, Taylor argues that there is no "objective, neutral thing" we call reason.[3] To assume that every person, from every tribe and nation, will come to similar conclusions about truth, love, meaning, and even logic by using this so-called neutral reasoning process is naïve and ethnocentric. This is a positive example of the postmodern critique on scientific reason. In his critique of the objective nature of reason, Taylor examined the real psychological and existential needs that are at play when our beliefs, be they Christian or secular, are threatened.

Let's look at the example of politics. Watch most any news event and flip channels between CNN and Fox News as they cover the same thing. You have broadcasters, experts, and eyewitnesses talking about the same event but coming up with radically different interpretations of the event. Both the CNN and Fox groups are intelligent, went to the same schools, and served in the same government, but they see things almost completely differently. Both say "Look at the evidence" or "Just be reasonable" or "Here are the facts" about this or that. So the idea that our reasoning powers are neutral or unbiased is simply not the case. We hold different political perspectives for different reasons, and these reasons will affect the way we view and interpret events.

How much more is this true when it comes to God and issues surrounding religion? How can we approach God reasonably? Without bias? Is this possible? Our reason, according to the Bible, has been tainted, distorted—fallen, if you will. So all people know that there is a God, but what they do with that information is entirely different.

As I mentioned earlier, the Bible teaches in Romans 1 that every person has a clear knowledge of God through the witness of nature. We know there is a God who made everything. But we take this obvious knowledge of God and suppress it because we want to run our own lives.

James Spiegel, in his book *The Making of an Atheist*, unmasks the feigned neutrality of atheists like Richard Dawkins and Sam Harris by showing that their decision to reject the existence of God is more about the will than the intellect.[4] Most individuals who say they're atheists will run quickly to science or reason as a cover for their unbelief. However, so many atheists reject God not because of lack of evidence but because of a willful choice. At least some atheists, like New York University philosophy professor Thomas Nagel, are honest about it. He admits:

> I speak from experience being strongly subject to this fear of religion myself. I want atheism to be true and am made uneasy by the fact that some of the most intelligent and well-informed people I know are religious believers. It isn't just that I don't believe in God and naturally hope

> that I'm right in my belief. It's that I hope there is no God. And I don't want there to be a God and I don't want the universe to be like that.[5]

Searching for Certainty in Science

The limitations of our reason are found not only in religion but in science as well. Here's what one noted physicist said about what scientists call the Heisenberg uncertainty principle:

> The uncertainty principle protects quantum mechanics. Heisenberg recognized that if it were possible to measure the momentum and position simultaneously with greater accuracy, then quantum mechanics would collapse. So, he proposed that it must be impossible. Then, people sat down and tried to figure out ways of doing it, and nobody could figure out a way to measure the position and the momentum of anything—a screen, an electron, a billiard ball, anything—with any greater accuracy. Quantum mechanics maintains its perilous, but accurate existence.[6]

Nobel Prize–winning physicist Steven Weinberg explained it this way: "We don't believe in quarks because we've seen them.

We believe in quarks because the theories that have quarks in them work."[7] We would say the same thing about faith. We don't believe in Christ because we've seen Him. We believe in Christ because, when we trust in Him, life seems to work and we have a lot of joy. That's my paraphrase of 1 Peter 1:8.

The Heisenberg uncertainty principle clearly illustrates how often we overlook the "little faiths" we believe in every day. Bell's theorem and Gödel's theorem (which apply to physics and mathematics respectively) illustrate the same idea. It amuses me to no end that we will develop complex theorems with complex names—theorems that basically say, "We don't know how these things happen. They seem impossible. But, you know what? They really do happen." And for some reason, this is easily accepted in the hard sciences but not in religion.

What does this mean to us? My reason can only take me so far. My reason, your reason, Stephen Hawking's reason are simply limited. We always bump into paradoxes, antinomies, and contradictions when we push our reason to the limit. We find paradoxes in astronomy, biology, physics, and mathematics. These realities perplex us and boggle our minds. They are inexplicable even to the experts. We are still unable to figure it all out. That's why we have the Heisenberg uncertainty principle, Gödel's theorem, etc. Society has passively accepted and embraced these academic conundrums that cannot be resolved with our reason alone.

When it comes to God, these principles also apply. God says our reason is good but not pure. Our reason is tainted.

Our reason is fallen. It's broken to the point where we take the obvious knowledge of who God is and suppress it. Why do we readily accept antinomies, anomalies, and paradoxes in the sciences? Maybe because quantum physics doesn't tell us to stop sleeping with our girlfriend. Bell's theorem doesn't say to stop partying and getting wasted. Heisenberg doesn't call you out for cheating on your taxes and fudging numbers to your clients. Unguided, random chaos and chance doesn't demand that you stop living a selfish life and start living for others. But God does. Who wants God to exist when we want to run our own lives?

Reason takes you only so far in life, whether you are talking about seeking religious truth or scientific truth. Everyone is just human: the scientist, the comedic cynic, and the preacher. We want to call our own shots. We don't look at all the evidence in a detached, unbiased way. We are not objective. Mathematician and philosopher Blaise Pascal said, "The supreme function of reason is to show man that some things are beyond reason."[8]

Taylor argued that "when people defend their world view, they are not defending reason or God, or an abstract system; they are defending their own fragile sense of security and self-respect."[9] In other words, we are all too human. We hunger for certainty like a starving man hungers for food. It's a part of who we are. Atheist and Christian fundamentalists will be there for you, willing to serve up another bowl of certainty, if that's what you want. Daniel Taylor helped me push away from the table.

I still believe in the fundamentals of the faith, but it has taken on an entirely different flavor. Taylor wrote, "Where there is doubt, faith has its reason for being. Clearly faith is not needed where certainty supposedly exists, but only in situations where doubt is possible, even present."[10] Faith helps us see God and interpret His world more clearly. It fills the many gaps in our knowledge about Him.

I know that I'm a little slow, but Taylor helped me finally realize that God desires trust from me, not certainty. That was a light-bulb moment. If I have certainty, then why do I need God or to trust in Him? Faith presupposes doubt. I may occasionally have psychological certainty, but that is not the same thing as an ironclad certainty about God, science, or whatever subject we feel can be proven without a doubt.

In addition, the idea that I can live my life without faith is preposterous. In his book *The Reason for God*, Tim Keller says that to doubt anything means you are exercising faith or belief in something else. In other words, there's always faith inherent in your doubt. When you doubt that God exists, you are simultaneously exercising faith in God's nonexistence in order to get your doubt going in the first place. If I doubt God is there, I am expressing faith that He is not there. I don't have proof. Keller challenges the doubter to see the faith inherent in their own doubts and to require just as much evidence for the new beliefs that you did for the old beliefs.[11]

I chose to stop chasing after the myth of objective certainty, some doubt-free existence, and to move forward in faith with this God who invites us into the uncertainties of life and existence.

Looking For a Knock-Down Argument

Sir John Polkinghorne is a noted theoretical physicist who mathematically explained the existence of quarks and gluons. He has a PhD in physics from Cambridge. Unlike physicist Steven Weinberg, Polkinghorne believes in God and in the death, burial, and resurrection of Jesus Christ. Polkinghorne still has doubts about God the same way he has doubts about his scientific research; however, he doesn't allow these doubts to prevent him from moving forward with God or with particle physics. He knows that his belief in God is a reasonable position, "but not a knock-down argument." Polkinghorne embraces the tension between certainty and uncertainty. He holds that the Christian faith is strong enough to bet your life on but that it cannot be proved beyond a shadow of a doubt.[12]

I have strong convictions about God and Christ. I am confident His Word is true. There is ample intellectual, archaeological, and historical evidence that undergirds our faith. We have a foundation. We are not just leaping into the dark or believing in fairy tales any more than an atheist or agnostic is. There is a place for these kinds of arguments and debates. Again, I've written books on this subject and will continue to teach courses on the validity of using intellectual means to communicate the faith.

I am not against reason or logic. I frequently remind people not to park their brains when they walk through the doors of a church. We have a rich, historical, and intellectual tradition in the Christian faith: from Athanasius to Augustine. From Pascal to

Kierkegaard. From Dostoyevsky to Lewis. The best and brightest minds flow from this river called the Christian faith. At the same time, skeptics and other philosophers have their heritage too. From Aristotle to Marcus Aurelius. From Buddha to Voltaire. From Nietzsche to Camus. I continue to learn from the skeptics as well. Some of Voltaire's insights to the problem of evil and suffering in his book *Candide* are unforgettable. Nietzsche's raw dismantling of science's so-called certainty is also helpful. However, the idea that reason can achieve certainty is an overreach for believers and non-believers. Our reason, both fallen and redeemed, is simply limited. We see in a mirror dimly, and we know only in part.

On a practical level, I needed to let go of this idol of certainty that I'd clung to for so long. I thought true faith—real faith—involved figuring it all out, having all the answers for myself and for anyone who would ask. But that's not the case. Author Jeanne Guyon, who suffered greatly in her life with loss and even incarceration, explained it like this: "If knowing answers to life's questions is absolutely necessary to you, then forget the journey. You will never make it, for this is a journey of unknowables—of unanswered questions, enigmas, incomprehensibles, and, most of all, things unfair."[13]

The Rest of the Story

The rest of the Kavanaugh and Mother Teresa story played out like this. When she told him that clarity (certainty) was the last thing he was holding on to and must let go of, Kavanaugh responded, "You always seem to have clarity." Teresa laughed and said, "I have never had clarity. What I have always had is trust. So I will pray that you trust God."[14] My prayer is that you will trust God in a deeper way as well. At the same time, trust must have an objective, a foundation on which to build. That's where we will pick up in the next chapter.

Chapter 9

Burning Down the House

"Merely having an open mind is nothing. The object of opening the mind, as of opening the mouth, is to shut it again on something solid."

G. K. Chesterton

When I was a little boy, our house burned down. Nothing was left except the chimney, which made our house look like a crude version of the Washington Monument. Thankfully, we had not moved into the house yet, but we were preparing to do so. I remember crying to my mom and feeling so angry that someone would burn our house to the ground. After the smoke cleared, my father surveyed the damage with our builder, Ralph Bagnell. Ralph felt the fire was so severe that we needed to dig up the old foundation and lay a brand-new one in order to build again. We did just that. And slowly but surely, we rebuilt the house that became my childhood home.

After many years of battling doubt and uncertainty, I felt like my faith had been burned to the ground. My certainty was charred, and my pride had been incinerated. Not much was left, but there was something or someone inside of me that said, *You must rebuild.* However, I realized that before I could rebuild, I had to lay down a new foundation for my house of faith. But what would my new foundation be? How could it withstand continual battles with doubt and uncertainty? I was basing my entire life on these beliefs, and my footings had to be solid. Slowly but surely, I began to rebuild my faith, starting with the foundation.

Jesus concluded the most famous speech delivered in the history of mankind, the Sermon on the Mount, by emphasizing the absolute necessity of a strong faith foundation. In Matthew 5–7, He laid out a myriad of challenging commandments that His followers must obey: Love your enemies. Pray for those who persecute you. Forgive those who hurt you. Turn the other cheek. Give your money away, but don't tell anybody you did it. Don't worry. Don't judge other people. Then He wrapped up this speech with a few parables that have rattled my cage for years. He said the way to heaven is narrow and the path to destruction is broad and how not everyone who says "Lord, Lord" will make it into paradise on judgment day. Then, He talked about the two foundations.

We are all building a life. And there are two types of builders—those who build their lives on a foundation of sand and those who build their lives on a foundation of rock. Christ said that hurricane-like storms will strike your life—wind, rain, and floods. The house built on the sand will be demolished, but the house built on the rock will survive. What's the difference? Those with the strong foundation dig deep, through the sand, all the way down to the rock.

As Americans, we love the silver-bullet moment that solves all the tension in a story. The hero beats up the villain and wins the day. The minor-league player pulled up for game seven of the World Series hits the game-winning home run. The overlooked maiden wins the hand of the charming young prince and they live happily ever after. Or in the case of doubt, the once-skeptical, now-seeking atheist discovers that the resurrection of Christ really did happen and all of his doubts vanish in a flash. I wish that were my story of dealing with doubt, but it's not. My story has been a long, drawn-out journey of highs and lows, receiving a hint here and discovering a clue over there. It's been a process. I have done a lot of digging.

So what constitutes a solid foundation? If you've ever driven on a road that cuts right through the side of a mountain, you may have noticed that the cross section of the slope reveals layers and layers of different types of rock, reaching down into the earth and built up over thousands of years. That's the kind of foundational strength we need to hold up a house of faith. For me, there are some important layers that make up my new and (hopefully) improved foundation.

Rebuilding the Foundation

The Personal Layer

On November 22, 1963, three major leaders in the Western world died—John F. Kennedy, Aldous Huxley, and C. S. Lewis. Obviously, Kennedy's assassination overshadowed the deaths of Lewis and Huxley, but in a tribute to all three men, philosopher Peter Kreeft wrote a book called *Between Heaven and Hell*. This book imagines what would happen if Kennedy, Huxley, and Lewis met somewhere "between heaven and hell" and had a discussion about the existence of God, Jesus Christ, and the mysterious religions of the East. As these three men engage in an amazing dialogue about life's ultimate concerns, Kreeft, speaking through the voice of C. S. Lewis, says that Christianity boils down to one critical issue. Lewis claims there is one central issue, one universal password, one skeleton key that can unlock every door.

Awhile back, I was preparing to teach a Sunday school lesson on some subject from Jeremiah 11. At the same time I was studying for this teaching, I was reading *Between Heaven and Hell* and became enraptured by this one critical issue. I continued to study for Jeremiah 11, and I eventually had a standard lesson prepared. But as Sunday drew near, I couldn't get this one central theme out of my mind. So here's what happened on Sunday.

I felt like I had to change my lesson for that day. My friend Mark Poe was the director of the class, and faithfully, every Sunday morning at eleven o'clock, he would welcome the class, give some announcements, and introduce the teacher. Right before class started, all I told Mark was, "It's going to be a little different today." That was a great understatement, but I didn't want to give it away. This was the most difficult speech of my life. It had to encapsulate the critical issue Lewis harped on in that book, which just might be the critical issue of the entire Bible: the universal password, the Theory of Everything. I slowly made my way to the lectern, looked out to the class, and shakingly uttered this simple but deep three-word phrase: "Jesus. Is. God." That's all I said. I stood there behind the podium, paused, and just let those three words hang in the air. I bowed my head. Trembling. No one said a word. Maybe some coughs. Then I sat down at a chair by the podium. No one said a word. We made it to lunch early that Sunday. Jesus is God. That is the critical issue.

Jesus. Jewish Messiah. Lived. Died. And rose again. Claimed to be God in the flesh. Men and women gave their lives for this belief. This is the personal aspect of Christianity that's helped me manage my doubt. He did come. He did die. He did rise. My feelings, my doubts, my fleeting thoughts do not change that reality one iota. This personal element is critical. And when you strip it all away, it comes down to the bold claim that Jesus is God. That's the reality that makes the Christian faith different from all others. Moses did not make such a claim. Muhammad did not make such a claim. Buddha never made this claim. How in the world can a human be divine? That's too big of a leap. It's impossible to hold those two seemingly contradictory truths simultaneously.

Take a look at the nature of light for a moment. Scientists have proven that light consists of particles, and they have the empirical data to back it up. Scientists have also proven the opposite—that light consists of waves—and they have the empirical data to back this up too. How can both be right? We don't know, but we hold to the reality that they are. This analogy applies to our belief in the person of Christ. How can He be both God and man at the same time? I cannot explain it, but that's what the data shows. I keep this antinomy and do not attempt to reconcile it.

Of course, you could look at it from another angle. Perhaps God becoming man was really no big deal. In other words, if there is an all-knowing, all-powerful God who exists far above time and space, how hard would it be for this God to enter into His creation for a moment of time? Some movie directors will often take off the director's hat and enter the story as an actor. On a much greater level, if God wanted to enter the story of mankind through becoming a man, what's the big deal? It may be a big deal to us, but it may not be a big deal to God.

I could walk you through the different options and reinterpretations of this claim—Jesus is God—but that is not the purpose of this book. Other gifted writers and historians like N. T. Wright, Gary Habermas, and C. Stephen Evans have done a much better job of that than I could. But all Catholic, Orthodox, and Protestant Christians unite on this pivotal, critical issue that Jesus Christ was and is God in the flesh. It's a bold claim. It's a game changer. It's as close to the Theory of Everything that you get. At the same time, this monumental, personal layer is inextricably tied to another layer in my foundation: the historical layer.

The Historical Layer

If you want to dig down deep to the foundations, Christianity relies on a strong historical layer tied to this radical rabbi, Jesus Christ. When the gospel writers situate the story of Jesus Christ within the first century during the time of the Roman Empire, they list the political leaders who were in charge and the cities, the towns, and the customs of the people who lived in that time period. This history tells the story of their encounters with a man named Jesus of Nazareth. Who was Jesus? What did He do? Why is that important to me?

I can look at the history of the New Testament, and it helps me answer those questions. I can read skeptics like Tacitus and Josephus who also help answer these historical questions. I can venture out into the second and third centuries and read

Ignatius, Origen, Justin Martyr, and critics like Celsus, and they also help answer these questions. Even if the New Testament was never written down in a book, the facts of the story remain.

Our faith claims that this One Man has lived in Ultimate Reality and in our temporal reality as well. "Jesus is Lord" was the claim of the first followers of Christ, and that's still the claim today. This claim is grounded in the history of the New Testament, in the early church fathers, and even in the critics of the Christian faith. When you investigate the key facts of the life of Christ, you are forced into an either/or choice. Either He did rise again, or He did not. Either He is God in the flesh, or He is not.

Princeton scholar B. B. Warfield put it like this:

> A God who is only an idea, and who never intervenes in the world of fact, can never actually save a soul that is real from sin that is real. For the actual salvation of an actual sin-stricken soul we require an actual Redeemer who has actually intervened in the actual course of history.... Christianity is a historical religion, all of whose doctrines are facts. He who assaults the trustworthiness of the record of the intervention of God for the redemption of the world, is simply assaulting the heart of Christianity.[1]

Of course, you cannot prove that a certain person in history was actually God. That cannot be proved beyond a shadow of a doubt. But it can be proved that this claim was made by a certain person, at a certain time, and was believed by a certain group of people. Therefore, my Christian faith is grounded in time-space history. Christianity is the good news about what God did through the person of Jesus Christ some two thousand years ago. Along with 2.3 billion other Christ followers, I have a personal historical conviction that this is what happened. This objectively happened or it did not. My foundation has a personal and a historical layer, but you might be asking how these layers help combat doubt and uncertainty. We have to get practical.

The Practical Layer

I have lived a lot of my life *inside* of my head. But truth is actually found *outside* of you and me. The gospel is about what God did for us in Christ some two thousand years ago on a hill outside of the city of Jerusalem. This objectively happened. There is nothing I can do to change it. My doubting the Christ event doesn't change its reality any more than my doubting oxygen would negate the fact that I am breathing it through my lungs at this very moment.

Philip Melanchthon, protégé of Martin Luther, was obsessed about his own salvation. He constantly worried and doubted whether he was saved or not. He fixated on any little sin that might cause God to stop loving him. He wrote Luther long letters chronicling his back-and-forth feelings of being "in" one day and "out" the next. Melanchthon simply had no peace.

Eventually, Luther came to his wits' end with Melanchthon's constant fretting and wrote him back: "Philip, go out and sin boldly and believe in Christ more boldly still. The gospel is completely outside of you."[2] That one phrase by Luther—"The gospel is completely outside of you"—began to slowly change my life and assuage my own doubt. What did Luther mean?

In today's language, he was saying, "It's not about you!" The gospel story is an actual event that happened two thousand years ago in Christ. He lived. He died. He rose again. Those are the facts. In His living, dying, and rising, Christ paved the way for us to be forgiven and accepted by God. He paid the price on the cross and lived a perfect life of righteousness in His obedience to God. Therefore, my righteousness is outside of me. I am 100 percent righteous before God. You are 100 percent righteous before God.

On a practical level, when I worry and fret as Melanchthon did—*Am I saved? Am I really a Christian? Have I done enough? What about this sin, and that sin?*—all of that is on the *inside.* Truth must come from the *outside*. The gospel is external to me. My righteousness is external to me. As Jesus said on the cross, "It is finished." It is done. The gospel on some level has nothing to do with me at all. That's freedom. It's not based on my good-day performances or my bad-day failures. It's based on the reality of what Christ did for me two thousand years ago in time-space history. It's objective and outside of me. It does not change based on my feelings and doubts. Peace comes when I look outside of myself to the cross. Lately, when someone asks me, "Well, when did you get saved?" I respond, "Two thousand years ago on a cross outside of Jerusalem." I trust in what someone did for me years ago to forgive me and set me free.

The same principle applies to being an American. I trust in what others did for me years ago to pave the way for the freedom I enjoy today. I did nothing. I trust in what they did to provide a free country. I rest in the realities that I am American because of what others did for me way before I came on the scene. All of my doubt and uncertainty about how our founding fathers did it is irrelevant to the fact that they did in fact accomplish it. I am free. I can rest in what they have done for me. However, many times our thoughts and emotions want to pull us the other way.

What if you woke up one day and said, "I don't feel married today"? Now, you've been married for twenty-five years. You have a wedding ring on the third finger of your left hand and three kids tucked in their beds down the hall. But for some reason, that morning you woke up and just didn't feel married. You go into a panic. "Why don't I feel married? Did I really say those vows twenty-five years ago? What happened?" So you go to see your pastor. You confess to him these strange feelings and thoughts you are having. He looks at you and says, "Hey, you are married whether you feel like it or not. Here's your marriage license. I signed it. I was there. I pronounced you man and wife. You are married, and that is the reality!" I can't help humming that old Boston song "More than a Feeling" right now.

That's a silly story, but it has helped me a lot when dealing with my doubt. I may wake up one morning and feel like God is not there. I may doubt that I am really a Christian. But that does not change the reality that I am in fact a Christian. God really did come to earth in Christ and die on a cross and rise again. My feelings and doubts in those moments don't change the reality of who God is and what He's done for me. I can choose to relax and trust in a God who's outside of me. I can trust what He did to forgive me and make me acceptable in His sight.

Dietrich Bonhoeffer, in his classic work *Life Together*, stated that a Christian sees his acceptance before God *in Jesus Christ alone, not in our feelings*. Bonhoeffer said, "He knows that God's Word in Jesus Christ pronounces him guilty, even when he does not feel his guilt, and God's Word in Jesus Christ pronounces him not guilty and righteous, even when he does not feel that he is righteous at all."[3] That's a solid foundation and a source of comfort when you are assailed by doubts.

My foundation has key layers: the personal layer, the historical layer, and the practical layer. As strong as these layers are, there must be a fourth layer. It's the layer that Jesus talked about when He encouraged us to build a rock-solid foundation. We might agree that the statement "Jesus is God" is true, historically grounded, and important, but that's simply not enough to complete the foundation. There is a mammoth difference between believing that "Jesus is God" and believing *in* Jesus. That's what the fourth layer is all about. For the application of this layer, we must turn to the brilliant and enigmatic philosopher Søren Kierkegaard.

The Experiential Layer

Kierkegaard helped me realize that the Christian life is a lived experience and not a thought experiment. In other words, following Christ is not something that you think about but something that you do. You can't think about faith and exercise faith at the same time. As C. S. Lewis scholar Clyde Kilby once said, "You can't think about kissing a girl, and kiss a girl at the same time."[4] A kiss is to be experienced, not thought about when you are in the moment. A Christian is a way of being in this world, not a set of doctrines and dogmas. It is a way of existing, a way of life. We are not brains in a jar, minds trapped inside bodies. We are human beings, wondrously designed with emotions, and that will play a tremendous role in our lives.

I think. I feel. I choose. I remember. I move. I see. I hear. I touch. I taste. I desire. I love. I doubt. I seek. I believe. I question. I commit. I know. I don't know. I desire. I dream. I imagine. I wonder. I hope. I bet. I guess. I yearn.

I marvel at beauty. I fear death. I endure suffering. I feel pain. I seek meaning. I enjoy music. I work hard. I hope for my kids. I feel happy. I am afraid. I grieve losses. I worry about the future. I get angry. I believe in God. I trust in Him. I surrender my life.

I want to be certain. I try to be helpful. I feel pain that pierces my soul with infinite remorse. But I live with much uncertainty. I launch out and I trust. I hold back and I cower. I feel so helpless.

Kierkegaard put it like this:

> Without risk there is no faith. Faith is the contradiction of a person's inward spirit and objective uncertainty. If I were capable of grasping God objectively, I would not believe. But since I cannot grasp him objectively I must believe. If I wish to persevere in my faith, I must constantly be intent on holding fast objective uncertainty, so in the objective uncertainty I am swimming in deep water—and yet believe.[5]

Though I do not fully grasp the depth of this quote, it still informs me about this mysterious relationship I have with God. If I could grasp God objectively, He would not be God. True faith is always risky business. And following God is always fraught with uncertainty and insecurity, like swimming in the depths of the ocean.

Kierkegaard engages the entire human experience. This fourth layer of our foundation may be the most important one: the layer of experience. We must engage in a Christianity that has solid personal, practical, and historical layers and, at the same time, is tethered to a vibrant, ongoing experience with God.

Søren Kierkegaard was one of seven children who grew up in an affluent Danish home in Copenhagen during the 1800s. By age seventeen, he could read Hebrew, Greek, French, German, Latin, and his native tongue of Danish. In spite of his privileged upbringing, Kierkegaard endured much pain in his life. By age twenty-five, he had buried not only five of his siblings but his mother and father as well. He suffered with a crippled body and battled depression throughout his life. He never enjoyed the fame and influence that would be lauded upon him posthumously, but instead he felt the continued ridicule and persecution of his own Danish people. A broken engagement with the love of his life, Regine Olsen, also shaped his life and writings in a profound way. He never fully recovered from that devastating breakup.

After his death, his writings were discovered and circulated around the world. He is known as the "father of existentialism," which is a philosophical point of view that has probably shaped every movie, novel, and play anyone has experienced in the last seventy years in the Western world. Existentialism looks at our humanity straight in the eye and says, "One day you are going to die, and in light of your impending death, how will you choose to authenticate yourself in this one and only life you will live? Make a choice." Though his writings have influenced the secular world in a profound way, his main goal in life was to influence the Christian church and share a better way to follow Jesus Christ.

I love Kierkegaard because he taught me how to follow Christ with my heart, my mind, and my will. I'm well aware of the pitfalls and shortcomings of Kierkegaard, and I do not endorse everything he said. Someone wisely told me years ago, "When you eat fish, remember to spit out the bones." I practice that same advice when reading a book or following someone as prolific as Kierkegaard. Having said that, his works rescued me from this fixation with certainty and launched me into the risky business that is this life of faith. He helped me get out of my head: to stop thinking about faith and to start living it.

When Faith Becomes a Real-Life Experience

Faith is something you do. Faith is trusting. Faith is not some cognitive construct. Obviously, I believe there is a cognitive and rational aspect of our faith. Of course. The Bible says, "Come now, let us *reason*" (Isaiah 1:18 ESV). "Love the Lord your God … with all your *mind*" (Matthew 22:37). Provide a "*reason* for the hope that you have" (1 Peter 3:15). I get that. But faith is about taking action based on what God has said. God desires that we experience His love, grace, and forgiveness. God calls us to follow Him in the way we live our lives.[6] That's the crucial difference. That's what will determine if we will weather the hurricanes and various storms that hit our lives. It's all about how we live it out; how we respond to His call, His voice, His grace.

Kierkegaard pounded this reality into my mind and soul. Doctrines about God, systematic theology, apologetics—all of these intellectual endeavors must be connected to a passionate real-time commitment to Christ.

Faith is all about trusting Christ in the present, not overthinking Christ in the past. Yes, in one sense I was saved two thousand years ago because of what Christ did for me in His living, dying, and rising, but I must experience this Christ in my own life, right now, in this moment. The *what* of our beliefs is important, but *how* we live them out is equally important, if not more important.

Everything is temporal. Nothing in this life lasts forever. I'm going to die. You're going to die. I am absolutely certain that we are all going to die. Benjamin Franklin said it: there are two certainties in this life—death and taxes. But very few people know when they will breathe their last breath. We *live* in denial of our deaths. Not only that, but we *act* like we are going to live forever. *I know everyone else has died before me. But somehow I'm going to beat this thing. I eat organic food, drink smart water, and do yoga. Heck, I'm gluten-free! I will live forever.* This is what's driving a lot of the fitness and health movement, as if there is a way to beat this thing called death. Won't happen. Death wins. Every time. This side of heaven, death is still undefeated.

I watched an interview with Dr. Stephen Liben, a palliative-care doctor in Montreal who treats children who are terminally ill. Liben talked about his call and challenge to care for children who will certainly die. He said, "We're all going to die. All of us. And the big question is, *How will you live, knowing that you will one day die?*" I don't know Dr. Liben's philosophical or religious perspective, but I do know he summed up the whole of existential thought in that one question.

For years, the church has always asked the question, "If you were to die today, where would you go?" And that is an important question, no doubt. But I think the question that we need to ask today is, *How are we going to live in the here and now, knowing that one day we will die?*

After I waded through all of my doubts, worries, and fears, I realized that to know how to answer that question, I had to resolve my beliefs about God. I had to buy in to the Jesus story. I had to decide to follow Him. And that's what I did. I am all in.

I will never figure it all out. I still have thousands of questions, but so what? This foundation of personal history and personal experience is real. Plus, I like Jesus Christ. He is the face of God to me. I need Him to forgive me and to empower me to live this one life. I bet it all on Him and His grace. Christianity is not my crutch; it's my entire life-support system, and the church is my hospital. I'm sick with sin and need a real doctor who can save me. Sue me. What will happen after death? I do not know for sure, but I desire to be with Him. I trust He took the sting of death away from me.

As I look at where I am today and where I was years ago, my doubts have changed. I met with a guy recently who was dizzy in doubt. I remember what that feels like. The anxiety. The pain. The dread. The sense that you want to believe in God but just still have these doubts. I understand. He asked me if I still doubted, and I told him I do but that I manage my doubt differently today than when I was sliding on the ice years ago.

If you are in a place where you are ready to dig deep and lay a new foundation, let me encourage you thoughtfully and prayerfully to consider the four layers I talked about in this chapter. I still go back to these four again and again in my own life when doubts and questions fill my mind. This is how it plays out in my life, and perhaps it will help you.

When questions, doubts, and fears push me out onto the ice again, I will turn to one or all of the four layers of my foundation. Do I trust God became a man in Jesus Christ? Yes. That's what the historical story tells me. When I do not feel very spiritual or authentically Christian, where do I turn? I look outside of me to the objective events of the gospel, His death, burial, and resurrection, which earned for me a righteousness that's not my own. I look outside of myself and trust in what Christ did two thousand years ago to make me acceptable before God. My fleeting doubts and emotions do not change the objective reality of what He did. These emotions will pass. Today, this very moment, experientially, I ask this same Jesus Christ to live through me and to empower me to face the challenges of this new day. Can I explain how that works? No, I cannot, but I can know that He has given me this experiential grace to follow Him in the complexities of my modern life. And I join the 2.3 billion Christians on this planet right now, and those throughout the history of the church, to live it out together.

Can You Trust the Voice?

Dr. Francis Schaeffer was the first philosopher to influence my understanding of God and the Christian faith from an intellectual and personal perspective. In *The God Who Is There*, he tells the story about a treacherous hiking expedition that helps bring two of these foundational layers—history and experience—together for me.[7]

Imagine that a man hiking in the Swiss Alps is unexpectedly hit by a blinding snowstorm. He can't even see a foot in front of his face as he sits on a narrow ledge. Finally, in desperation, the man cries out, "Help! Is anyone out there?" In the cold, blustering storm he hears a voice, "Yes, I'm here. I can help. Just leap off the ledge to the path below." What if that was an unknown voice? Would the man trust the advice and take that leap? Maybe not. But suppose that the voice speaking out of the storm said, "I've hiked this mountain for thirty years and I know every inch of it. Just leap off the ledge you are on and you will land on a path that will lead you to safety." Would the man leap?

To expand this story a bit, think about how this man is simply one of many who've encountered such hazardous conditions on that same mountain. Would he have a better chance of leaping if he had heard the stories of many others who, equally lost, heard the same voice?

The Voice is God's voice. He calls out from history and from the experience of others and says, "Jump. You can trust Me. I will catch you and lead you on a good path. A path with a solid foundation."

I am thankful for that foundation and that good path I am traveling today, but what if you think you will never find that path? What if you are still wandering in the dense forest of doubt? Help is on the way. Turn the page.

Chapter 10

The Moon Is Round

"The opposite of faith is not doubt, but certainty. Certainty is missing the point entirely. Faith includes noticing the mess, the emptiness and discomfort, and letting it be there until some light returns."[1]

Anne Lamott

I am a recovering addict. My addiction isn't to alcohol or drugs; I'm recovering from an addiction to doubting. As I mentioned earlier, I am a grateful doubt-aholic. I am grateful because God taught me about faith, courage, and hope through all of my doubts. I am grateful for the people I've met because of my doubts and for the lives of fellow doubters I've learned from through the years. But it hasn't always been this way. Not at all.

If you've never been to an AA meeting, I encourage you to check one out. AA holds some "open meetings" that welcome anyone to come regardless if you are a recovering addict. The beauty and wisdom you will glean from attending a meeting by just sitting and listening will be vast. Here's what I've learned through attending a few meetings, reading the Big Book, and hanging out with my friends who are at various stages of recovery.

In an AA group, no one judges you based on your race, your education, your wealth. They don't care if you drove up in a Mercedes or just got out of prison. You may feel you are better and smarter than the people around you, but as the writer Stephen King says, "We all look pretty much the same when we're puking in the gutter."[2] The level of acceptance in most Twelve Step groups is like none other. Unconditional love and acceptance are what you will find. Everyone in the group has been to hell and back. They know what it feels like to "hit bottom" or "come to the end of your rope." No story of pain, loss, and chaos from a new guy rattles their chains because they've heard it all. Plus, the old-timers are living survival stories, examples to the newcomers who need hope. Just like in the story of the man stuck in the blizzard, they provide proof of men who went down the same path and made the jump.

AA is a simple program for complex people. Twelve Steppers know exactly the pain and frustration you are going through.

We have all been there. We have found that our addiction is a life-or-death situation, that we had to admit that we were powerless to overcome it, and that only God can restore us to sanity. We hit bottom because we have a big problem. We found that we can only overcome this big problem through the help of God and the people in the group. Millions of men and women have found the solution in the Twelve Steps. We've followed the program and are free. If you want to get free, we can help you. This is simply our testimony and the testimonies of millions of recovering addicts around the world who have kicked their addictions as well.

When I was stuck in the middle of my bout with doubt, I wished there had been a Twelve Step support group to attend—a place called Doubters Anonymous or something like that. I would have walked in and said, "Hi, my name is Ben, and I am a doubt-aholic." The group would reply in unison, "Hi, Ben." Then I would go on to tell my story of how I got drunk on doubt:

> I doubt that God is there. I doubt that the Bible is true. I'm more convinced of evolution than creation. I can't look at nature without thinking about evolution. I don't understand how God could become a man. I don't see why a person dying on a cross two thousand years ago has anything to do with me. I pray for a sign or a miracle and get nothing.

Then after I blathered on about all of my doubt, an old-timer in the Twelve Step group would say, "Yep, I get it." Then someone else would pipe up, "I was in that exact place two years ago. I know just how you feel." Then the group leader would say, "Ben, you've come to a safe place to doubt. We've been helping doubt-aholics like you for years. Hey, we're all doubt-aholics ourselves. Just work the program. We will give you a sponsor, and you can call him anytime of the day or night if you feel like your doubts are freaking you out. Thanks for sharing."

I know that may sound odd, but I wish there had been a place like that. And my desire is that this book would serve as a type of Twelve Step group for you. A place where you can go to reflect and connect with someone who knows what you are going through and can provide some help along the way.

The founders of AA were known as Bill W. and Dr. Bob. They were so smart. Though they'd had born-again experiences themselves, they realized other people may have had bad experiences in church or may not share their beliefs. Many folks had hang-ups even talking about God, Jesus, or Christianity. When people walked into a meeting for the first time, they didn't say, "You have to believe the Bible is true. You have to believe in a talking snake and a man renting a room inside a whale. You have to believe Jesus rose from the dead. You have to believe Jesus is God." Nope. That's not what they said.

Instead, they accepted people where they were. They said you simply have to be willing to admit that your life has become unmanageable. Turn your life over to a higher power or just pretend to believe. You don't take all twelve steps at once. Start with step one. Start where you are, not where you think you should be or where you want to be, but honestly where you are at this moment. Ask God to help you experience Him in a fresh way. Don't try to believe in this strange doctrine or supernatural miracle. Start with a simple confession of your brokenness and your desperate need in your life. Even if you don't believe God is real at this moment. Obviously, their approach is not for everyone, but I like the fact that they meet people right where they are.[3]

For years, my friend Mark was an outspoken atheist. He thought Christianity was nonsense. A highly educated and well-read person, he would mock Christians and their naïve beliefs about God. At the same time, he had a drinking problem that had gotten out of hand. He met a guy who told him to pray to God for help to stop drinking. Mark said, "I can't do that. I don't believe God exists, so how can I pray to someone that isn't real?"

The wise old man said, "Just pretend. When you wake up in the morning, ask this God you don't believe in to help you stop drinking, and at the end of the day thank Him for helping you not drink."

Mark thought the idea was silly, but he knew he needed help, so he took the advice of the older gentleman about prayer. As fate (God) would have it, he stopped drinking. Mark slowly began to believe in the existence of God, as he continued to gain freedom from alcoholism.

After many years of praying to God, he began seeking a real relationship with this God. He tried some Buddhism, but it did not work. He tried some Mormonism, but it did not work. He tried a myriad of self-help books, but they did not work either. Over time, he started to ask questions about the person of Jesus Christ. What did He teach? Why did He have to die on a cross? Who was He?

Gradually, Mark came to trust in Jesus Christ. He told me, "Ben, when I was an atheist, I had difficulty believing in the existence of any God. So back then, if you told me God had become a person in Jesus Christ, I would have said you were insane."

So start where you are with God. Come to Him as you are, doubts and all. That's where Mark started. Take the words of Dr. Martin Luther King Jr., who aptly said, "Faith is taking the first step when you don't see the whole staircase."

If you are in a season of doubt right now, what's your first step to deal with this doubt? Think about that or pray about it, even if you don't believe that prayer works for you. What's your first step? Maybe it's simply to acknowledge to a trusted friend or mentor, "I'm having doubts about my Christian faith." Maybe it's for you to pray to God like this: "I don't believe in You right now, but I want to believe in You." Or: "God, I am afraid I don't have enough faith to believe in You. Please help." Don't worry about the rest of the staircase.

Maybe evolution has you in a tizzy. Or you don't know how you can ever believe in the Trinity or any of the miracles in the Bible. Or you wonder how you can believe in God's love when

He allowed so much pain and tragedy into your life. Get simple. Live in this moment. Take the first step. Those issues you are struggling with may seem big, or maybe they are really big. I get it. However, ask God to help you with this first step. And then move to the next step and the next step, as you progress one day at a time up the staircase.

I hope you've found acceptance and a nonjudgmental friend as you've read through the pages of this book. I know we all have our own individual doubt stories, but I wanted to share with you a portion of my journey and some of my friends' journeys as well. I do not have twelve steps that will set you free from doubt. That's not really the goal. But I do want to share some final words that have been helpful to me and other doubt-alcoholics as they've processed their own doubts on the way to building a stronger faith.

Where Do We Go From Here?

You Are Not an Island

One of the most ineffective ways to deal with doubt is to keep it to yourself. Perhaps you think you can work this out on your own. But you probably cannot. One of the most effective ways to deal with doubt is to doubt out loud. In other words, you need to tell a trusted friend, mentor, or pastor about what you are battling. You will need someone else to guide you through this season and to help you deal with the nuances of doubt. It may take time to find the right person to help, but be patient and trust that such people will come into your life. Philip Yancey expressed his advice for finding a community for doubting in the following way:

> Inquisitiveness and questioning are inevitable parts of the life of faith. Where there is *certainty* there is no room for *faith*. I encourage people not to doubt alone, rather to find some people who are safe "doubt companions," and also to doubt their doubts as much as their faith. But it doesn't help simply to deny doubts or to feel guilty about them. After all, many people have been down that path before and have emerged with a strong faith.[4]

Yancey's idea of finding "doubt companions" is a helpful concept, as is his encouragement for the doubter to hold on to the truth that many have gone this way before and have ended up with strong faith.

Let's look back to the stories of Job, John the Baptist, and Thomas. Job voiced his doubt out loud to his misguided but well-meaning friends. John the Baptist voiced his doubts out loud to one of his disciples and actually sent his doubt directly to Jesus Himself. Thomas voiced his doubt out loud to his closest friends in direct fashion—"I will not believe it until I see it." It's essential that you talk to someone you can trust about your doubts.

You Are Normal

Almost everyone I've talked to who went through a season of doubt felt shame. Psychology explains that guilt stems from the fact that one has *done something* wrong, but shame says you *are* wrong.[5] If you are going through a period of doubt, you may feel out of place and full of shame. It is common to look around at your circle of friends who seem to have no struggles with doubt and feel as if you're abnormal. They seem to "get it," but you don't. You feel as though having doubts means that you're not a Christian. Or it means that if you are a Christian, then you are certainly not a good one. It feels as if most people do not wrestle with doubt. But you can rest assured that, although you may feel abnormal, you are not. In fact, the opposite is true. You are going through a very common and normal process.

Brennan Manning said, "But what about doubts and worries? Do they, too, signal a rejection of God's Kingdom? Not necessarily. There can be no faith without doubt, no hope without anxiety, and no trust without worry."[6] Allow your doubts to drive you to deeper faith. Remember the goal here is not "doubt-free living" but trusting God in the moment when you don't have all the answers.

You Are in Good Company

One of the greatest weapons the Enemy uses against us is isolationism. He wants you to believe that you are the only one in your group who struggles with doubt and that doubt is a very shameful activity to indulge in. That's a lie. So many people around you are struggling with doubt. You're not alone, my friend.

In fact, the Bible is loaded with doubters. Adam and Eve doubted. Abraham doubted. Moses doubted. David doubted. Elijah doubted. Habakkuk doubted. Job doubted. John the Baptist doubted. Peter doubted. Jesus doubted. Doubt is a part of the process for many Christians, and it is a part of being human.

Church history reveals that there is a long line of doubters in the Christian faith. Augustine, Luther, C. S. Lewis, and Mother Teresa all struggled with doubt. Many contemporary writers like Philip Yancey, Anne Lamott, Os Guinness, and Brennan Manning have written very candidly about their nagging doubts. Don't be deceived into thinking that you are alone in your doubts. There are doubters in the Bible. There are doubters throughout church history. There are doubters all around. Right now, you are reading words written by a gifted doubter.

Surrender to the Process

Because doubt can be so painful and relentless, it is easy to get frustrated when the doubt simply will not go away. Perhaps like me, you tried prayer, reading the Bible, or a great book on doubt. Nevertheless, the doubts stayed with you. They are still there.

You must refuse to worry, because for most people, dealing with doubt takes time. As difficult as it may seem, God may actually be doing a great work in your life in the process of your struggle. You might be thinking, *Well, how can that be? I don't even know if God really exists right now.* But God is bigger than your thoughts and doubts. Surrender to the process. It does not mean you should be passive. But it does mean you will have to let go of your timetable for overcoming doubts. Philosopher Robert Baird hints at the kind of work God might be up to in permitting this season of doubt:

> Most basic beliefs and value commitments are initially inherited from parents, peers, and society at large. If these beliefs and commitments are not challenged by creative doubt, they tend to become simply verbal professions having little vitality. Creative doubt stimulates the evaluation of beliefs. Beliefs found wanting may appropriately be discarded. Those found adequate may be reasserted with new vigor and life.[7]

This reevaluation of beliefs, with the discarding of inadequate ones, is an important way in which God purges us. You will lay a new foundation once you work your way through this, but in the meantime, it's important you surrender to this creative process.

Make Up Your Bed and Go to the Park

A friend of mine once told me that simply getting out of bed and going to take a walk at the park with a mentor helped him process his doubt. In spite of the benefits to doubt just mentioned, one of the biggest quagmires doubt creates is that it can force you to "live life in your head." You think you might explode because all these thoughts, ideas, Bible verses, and contradictions cannot be reconciled. Hours and days of your life can be spent not really living but instead thinking. Living inside your head.

It's what we looked at earlier that Martin Luther called *anfechtungen.* Here is a bit of his practical advice to fellow strugglers: "Be with people. Do not isolate yourself. Listen to music. Exercise. Drink. Have sex with your spouse. Wrestle with God like Jacob. Let a friend speak truth to you."[8]

Luther compared these remedies to putting one's trust in a doctor while sick. He said that sometimes a sick person feels he's getting sicker, while a doctor who understands the disease says, "No, you are actually getting better." Luther's advice is to trust the doctor. In other words, you should trust your friend and his or her counsel rather than your immediate thoughts and feelings.[9]

Befriend Razor-Sharp Doubt

I have a friend in Hawaii named Gavin. I call him the "Desert Son," and he calls me the "Desert Father." I met the Desert Son in a surf shop years ago. I was working on a book and doing research on second-century mystics who fled to the desert and became known as the Desert Fathers—hence the nicknames. I was a newbie surfer filled with questions and trepidations about surfing. When I first learned how to surf, I battled many fears. How do I avoid getting attacked by the sharks? How do I avoid getting hit by other surfers? How do I prevent the board from smashing me on the head? And then there was the reef. How do I avoid falling off my board and getting ripped to shreds on the sharp reef?

Gavin was born and raised on the island, so I asked him how to deal with my fear of the reef. He said, "Oh, I don't know. After a while, you just learn to develop a relationship with the reef."

As a rookie surfer, I thought that sounded a little Zen, a little crazy. But the longer I've surfed, the more I have come to understand what the Desert Son was trying to explain to me. Without the reef, you wouldn't have those perfect waves. Waves are created by the shape of the bottom of the ocean floor. Reefs are beautiful, colorful, brilliant, and alive … but on the other hand, they are also razor-sharp like a surgeon's scalpel. I have scars on my body from hitting the reef. So it's dangerous, but at the same time, the reef is the ecosystem that keeps the ocean alive, and it also provides the necessary contours to produce perfect waves that bring inexpressible and glorious joy to surfers. Now I understand what having a relationship with the reef is about. You respect it for its danger, and you enjoy it for its power and beauty.

Doubt is not unlike the reef. Doubt can hurt you, but it can also shape your faith. Doubt drove me to dig deep into the foundations of the Christian faith. Doubt introduced me to intelligent and wise Christian thinkers. Doubt caused a major crisis in my life, which opened up the door for my understanding of grace. Doubt made me a better student of life. Doubt helped me understand the questions of my skeptical friends and to be patient with them. Doubt delivered me from the search for certainty and pointed me in the direction of trust and faith. That's what befriending doubt did in my life.

Know That God Is Bigger Than Your Doubts

When a person battles with doubt, one of the biggest temptations is to internalize those doubts and not talk to God about them. It is better to doubt out loud, as Job and Thomas did. When looking at the stories of Job and Thomas, you will find two different people living in two different contexts dealing with two different kinds of doubt. Job's doubt came from the catastrophic loss he experienced, whereas Thomas's doubt came from his inability to trust his friends' account that Jesus had risen from the dead.

As different as these two men were, they both had the courage to doubt out loud. Job doubted to his friends and to God. As a matter of fact, Job raged against God. Thomas told his friends directly that he did not believe the news. He would need to see Jesus face to face for himself in order to believe. No matter how unpopular it was, both doubted out loud. God did not kick Job off the planet, and Jesus did not kick Thomas out of the small group either. God is bigger than your doubts, and He wants you to be candid with Him about them. It can also be helpful to journal as a part of this process. Both strategies get this doubt out in the open. If there is a God and He is all knowing, then you might as well state it out loud—for your own sake, not for God's.

God is not taken aback by the questions you have. They are not going to knock God off His throne. You are not going to somehow tip and mess up the equilibrium of the universe because you may have happened on this particular day to doubt whether God is really there or to doubt whether God can really intervene. That is not going to rock God's world. God is God. He is unchanging. He is the same yesterday, today, and forever. But get honest with God and know that He is really bigger than your doubts.

Remember That the Moon Is Round

A story of a fourteen-year-old girl made an impact on me. She had been battling cancer for many years. When she started the fight and began the grueling treatments, she kept a notebook. She journaled and kept scriptures in that notebook to encourage her along this journey that was filled with trials and suffering. The doctors did everything they could, but in time, she passed away.

After she went on to be with the Lord, her parents found a notecard in her journal. It was a simple notecard that had only four words on it: "The Moon Is Round." At first they couldn't figure it out. What did that phrase mean to her? Perplexed by the phrase, they went back and searched in her journal and started to read some entries she had reflected upon. She had written, "When things are dark and I can only see a sliver of the moon, I know that the moon is still round. When the cancer is so tough and the treatments are so brutal and I can only get a sliver—just a slice of the love, and the power, and the presence of God, I know that the moon is round. It's round."

God is real when we can't see Him, feel Him, or understand Him. He is there. He does love you right where you are. The moon is round.

Appendix

Can You Trust the Bible?

"It is not certain that everything is uncertain."
Blaise Pascal

Some skeptics believe the Bible is full of myths. However, this belief is not well founded when you look at the actual contents of the Bible. I mentioned Bart Ehrman several times in this book and how he left the Christian faith. Some of his skepticism came from seeing variances in the texts that throw some people off track.

However, there are so many conservative scholars, like Daniel Wallace, J. I. Packer, and Richard Pratt, who hold to inerrancy while understanding the variances in the text. I would put myself in the same camp. I hold to inerrancy while embracing the numerous yet insignificant variances. You don't have to go through a season of doubt and lose your trust in the Bible or your faith altogether. Check out the Chicago Statement on Biblical Inerrancy if you need detailed help explaining how minor variances do not affect the inerrancy of the Bible.

I wrote the following section to help Christians answer the claims of skeptics who say, "The Bible is full of myths," or "You can't believe the Bible because it contains miracle stories," or "Monks changed the words over the years of translating."

Not the Stuff Myths Are Made Of

First of all, if you were to say the Bible is full of myths, I would have to ask you what you mean by the word *myth*. If you have read the Bible and have studied classical literature at all, you have seen that the Bible is not written in a mythical style. Nor does it read like a fairy tale, which is highly fanciful. It reads like a record of history that contains a wide variety of literary genres—biography, poetry, narrative, and eyewitness accounts.

Let's take a moment to look more closely at one of these eyewitness accounts. See how realistic in nature John's account of the Pharisees and the adulteress is. These self-righteous men threw her at the feet of Jesus, testing Him to see if He would condemn this "obvious sinner." Instead of condemning her, the writer reported that Jesus quietly began writing in the sand. This is exactly what a true eyewitness would tell us—details he understood no more than we do. This is not the sort of detail that ends up in legends.

And what of the specific names and dates in the gospel accounts that place them on an actual timeline? (For example, Luke mentions a census that took place "while Quirinius was governor of Syria.") These are not characteristic of the vagueness of legends either. Consider all the little insights into character we get as well. Legends don't have such depth. If the Gospels are not genuine eyewitness accounts and are merely fantasy or legend, then not only did these Galilean commoners invent the biggest and most successful hoax in human history, but they also created a unique and unprecedented literary form—the realistic fantasy—and that is highly unlikely.[1]

Here's a thought: perhaps the reason people see the Bible as mythical is not because it has the characteristics of myths but because myths have the characteristics of the Bible.

Do You Believe in Miracles?

Most often, when people say they have a problem with the Bible because it seems mythical, what they are really saying is they have a problem with the supernatural—the parting of the Red

Sea, the virgin birth, the walking on water, and the raising of the dead (just to name a few). Skeptics say: "The Bible is basically a bunch of myths … miracles like that don't happen these days, and if they don't happen now, why would they have happened then?" In other words, "We now live in a modern, enlightened world, and everyone knows that miracles do not happen because they are contrary to the laws of nature."

How do you know miracles do not happen today? Let's think about this question for just a moment. How much information would you really need to make such a claim? How much data about the natural realm would you have to have at your disposal to know for a fact that miracles are impossible? The answer is obvious if you're intellectually honest with yourself: you would have to know every conceivable fact of science to make the grandiose claim that a supernatural world does not exist.

How do you account for the immutable laws of nature, given your worldview? How do you know that nature operates in a law-like manner? Perhaps you would answer, "I know nature obeys certain laws because I can see and test those laws." The first problem with that answer is this: not all of nature is contained in your minute experience. In philosophical argumentation, you are guilty of a *hasty generalization*, which means you are taking a tiny bit of evidence and universalizing it.

The second problem with your answer is a little more complicated: if all you can know is what you can see and test, then you really can know very little. Why? Because you cannot be sure the knowledge you take in at this present moment can be applied to the past or to the future. You may *assume* it applies, but you cannot *know*—because you can neither go back in time nor jump to the future to test it. This is one of the reasons atheistic philosopher David Hume said we cannot see causation (the relationship between causes and effects). In other words, you cannot determine that A necessarily causes B simply because B happens to follow A at a given point in time. You can see that B may follow A *most* of the time, but you cannot possibly know that it always has or always will.

You can learn a lot about the difference between causation and mere correlation from Lisa Simpson in this humorous scene that appeared in an episode of *The Simpsons*:

> Homer: Not a bear in sight. The "Bear Patrol" must be working like a charm!
>
> Lisa: That's specious reasoning, Dad.
>
> Homer: Thank you, dear.
>
> Lisa: By your logic, I could claim that this rock keeps tigers away.
>
> Homer: Oh, how does it work?
>
> Lisa: It doesn't work.
>
> Homer: Uh-huh.
>
> Lisa: It's just a stupid rock. But I don't see any tigers around, do you?
>
> Homer: Lisa, I want to buy your rock.[2]

If you cannot see causation, then you cannot say with any authority that there are certain laws nature has always and will always obey. Therefore, to reason that you can know that miracles are impossible simply because Mother Nature follows certain rules is completely arbitrary, given your inability to account for these rules. The truth is, in order to do science or math, or even think and argue logically, you need an omniscient and omnipresent God who providentially controls and guides the universe in a predictable way.[3]

Have Monks Morphed the Texts?

A common argument skeptics use to cast doubt on the reliability of the Bible is to say it has been "embellished" over the centuries. Maybe you agree with them and would say to me: "How can you be sure the Bible you have today is the original? Surely the scribes and monks who made copies of the original manuscripts changed the texts through the years, and therefore, no one can really know for sure if it contains the true words of Christ." Well, do you have evidence to back your claim? What if I said I didn't think Mark Twain really wrote *Huckleberry Finn* and accused him of plagiarizing the whole thing? I can make that argument all day long, but it is mere opinion if I don't provide you with evidence. Where is the evidence that medieval monks tampered with the original?

Furthermore, do you have any knowledge in the field of textual criticism? Here's what author and scholar Helmut Koester has to say on how the New Testament (NT) fits in that field:

> Classical authors are often represented by but one surviving manuscript; if there are half a dozen or more, one can speak of a rather advantageous situation for reconstructing the text. But there are nearly five thousand manuscripts of the NT in Greek ... The only surviving manuscripts of classical authors often come from the Middle Ages, but the manuscript tradition of the NT begins as early as the end of [the second century AD]; it is therefore separated by only a century or so from the time at which the autographs were written. Thus it seems that NT textual criticism possesses a base which is far more advantageous than that for the textual criticism of classical authors.[4]

Let's look at Plato as an example of the type of classical author Koester is talking about. Does anyone doubt that the words we read from *The Republic* are indeed Plato's words? Probably not. What about the history of the manuscript? Well, Plato wrote it in about 355 BC, and the earliest manuscript we have is from AD 900. That's a gap of more than twelve centuries, for those of you keeping score at home.

Now, let's take the Scriptures, specifically the New Testament. It was written between AD 50 and AD 90, and the earliest manuscripts we have are from around the year AD 100. That's a gap of only fifty years at most. That's not a significant amount of time for tweaking of epic proportions—pun intended. (What would have been the monks' motivation anyway?) Here's what even a liberal scholar like John A. T. Robinson says about the credibility of Scripture: "The wealth of manuscripts, and above all the narrow interval of time between the writing and the earliest extant copies, make it by far the best attested text of any ancient writing in the world."[5]

The New Testament and the Old Testament—check out the Dead Sea Scrolls if you want more evidence—are reliable books of antiquity. Their historical credibility is verified not only through stout manuscript evidence but also through continuing archaeological discoveries that support the evidence for the lives of the people and the events mentioned in their pages.

Longevity and Reliability

And something must be said for the Bible's longevity. Look at what the *Times* of London said about it:

> Forget modern British novelists and TV tie-ins. The Bible is the best-selling book every year. If sales of the Bible were included in best-seller

> lists, it would be a rare week when anything else would achieve a look-in. It is wonderful, weird … that in this godless age … this one book should go on selling, every month.[6]

Further, the Bible has been translated more times and into *more* languages than any other book. Highly unlikely stats for a book with sketchy credibility, wouldn't you say? On top of all that, we could look at the Bible's amazing influence on political figures, thinkers, writers, emperors … you name it. Here are just a few examples:[7]

- *Abraham Lincoln*: "I believe the Bible is the best gift God has ever given man. All the good from the Saviour of the world is communicated to us through this book."
- *George Washington*: "It is impossible to rightly govern the world without God and the Bible."
- *Napoléon*: "The Bible is no mere book, but a Living Creature, with a power that conquers all that oppose it."
- *Daniel Webster*: "If there is anything in my thoughts or style to commend, the credit is due to my parents for instilling in me an early love of the Scriptures … If we abide by the principles taught in the Bible, our country will go on prospering and to prosper; but if

we and our posterity neglect its instructions and authority, no man can tell how sudden a catastrophe may overwhelm us and bury all our glory in profound obscurity."

- *Thomas Carlyle*: "The Bible is the truest utterance that ever came by alphabetic letters from the soul of man, through which, as through a window divinely opened, all men can look into the stillness of eternity, and discern in glimpses their far distant, long forgotten home."
- *Thomas Huxley*: "The Bible has been the Magna Carta of the poor and oppressed. The human race is not in a position to dispense with it."
- *Immanuel Kant*: "The existence of the Bible, as a book for the people, is the greatest benefit which the human race has ever experienced. Every attempt to belittle it is a crime against humanity."
- *Charles Dickens*: "The New Testament is the very best book that ever was or ever will be known in the world."
- *Sir Isaac Newton*: "There are more sure marks of authenticity in the Bible than in any profane history."

Either all these people were duped, or there is, indeed, something powerful about this book.

The Bible Is Bad Propaganda

There is one last argument I would like to make for the credibility of the Bible. Some say that the Bible is nothing more than a piece of propaganda that's been used by political figures throughout history to further their own agendas.

Here's why that line of reasoning does not work: The Bible makes a really bad piece of propaganda. The Scriptures are fraught with the many failures of its main characters and even heroes.

- We can start with Noah, who got drunk and passed out naked.
- There was Abraham, who lied about his wife being his sister on more than one occasion because he was afraid for his life.
- Moses was a murderer.
- David was an adulterer *and* a murderer.
- Solomon made pagan women his wives and lost his closeness with God.
- Judas—one of the original disciples—turned Jesus in for a meager thirty pieces of silver and then committed suicide.

- Peter denied Christ three times.
- Saul (later Paul) had followers of Jesus stoned to death while he looked on with approval.

And these are the guys who messed up. What about the innocent ones who were persecuted, sold into slavery, beaten, thrown to the lions, and even killed in some cases—like Abel, Joseph, Daniel, all the disciples … and Jesus Himself! A good piece of propaganda would not expose the faults of its so-called heroes, nor would it highlight the sufferings of those faithful to it.

Who Is Your Ultimate Authority?

All of us turn to an authoritative source for answers and information that will help us make sense of the world we live in. For the world of finance, many people turn to *The Wall Street Journal*. In the world of fashion, *Vogue* and *GQ* are respected authorities. When it comes to ultimate issues, perhaps your standard is empiricism ("Seeing is believing") or rationalism ("I think, therefore I am"). But whether you would define yourself as an empiricist or a rationalist, what you're ultimately saying is this: you are your own authority when it comes to deciding life's truths. As a Christian, I turn to the Bible as my authoritative source for answers about life.

As I write this, I can already hear your concern: "But why do you accept the Bible as the only divinely inspired book?

Why not accept the Koran or the Bhagavad Gita as well?" My response is twofold:

> 1. The Bible is uniquely inspired and, as such, presents a unique worldview. It claims to be God's very words, and it instructs us that other sources that contradict or distort these words are to be dismissed. This does not mean I cannot find some truth in Buddhism, Hinduism, or Islam. However, ultimate truth is found in God's once-and-for-all revelation to mankind: the Bible. I have yet to find a more complete, authoritative source for life and all of its complexity.
>
> 2. Jesus is my ultimate authority. He claimed to be God revealed in a person, so His words are more authoritative than those of any other religious leader. My belief in the authority of the Bible also stems from my faith commitment to Jesus Christ, who regarded the Scriptures as authoritative and commissioned His followers to pass on His message to all people, in all places.

So, everyone has a standard to which he or she turns in order to make sense of reality. My standard is the revelation of God, who has no other need for verification. (That's what makes God, *God.*) If there is a God who stands outside of temporal reality, then He has the ultimate interpretation on every fact in the known world and beyond. This does not mean that I, or any other Christian, have "all the answers," but it does mean we have placed our trust in Someone who does.

You may say this is a cop-out, but you can't avoid trust—it's a given everywhere around us and in everything we do. We are all believers—it's just a matter of who or what we choose to believe in. You may have noticed that throughout this book, I've refrained from using the terms *believers* and *unbelievers* to refer to Christians and non-Christians. Why? Because "doing so would encourage the totally erroneous notion that 'believing' or 'having faith' is something only some of us do," explains Michael Guillen, former ABC News science correspondent and theoretical physicist. "Truth is, every one of us 'believes.' Every one of us 'has faith.' What divides us are the different objects of our faith, our different gods."[8]

So suppose for a moment there is a God who rules everything and is the Creator—the Eternal, the All-powerful, and the All-knowing. Could you think of any higher authority than this God? What kind of God would He be if He needed a mere man or a mere man's philosophy to vouch for Him? He certainly wouldn't be very "God-like," would He? Therefore, wouldn't you expect this God to speak with self-attesting authority? Who else could authenticate His revelation to humans? How could any person know what this God would say and be like in order to confirm this revelation?

Really, it comes down to this: If you will not accept the Bible on its own terms, then what you are saying is that you will never accept a revelation from God. Only God, if He is God, could reveal Himself with final authority, and that is exactly what He does. So those who reject the Bible reject it not for reasons of hard evidence but simply because they have a different absolute measure by which they judge truth. I presuppose the Bible as my ultimate authority and foundation for truth, and they presuppose their own minds.

Let's take a breather and simplify for a moment. Questioning the authority or authenticity of the Bible is, for me, a little like deconstructing "Mary Had a Little Lamb." Think about it. We could all hone in on particular aspects and pose our questions. For example, how little was the lamb exactly? Was it really little or just little in comparison to Mary? Perhaps Mary is rather large. Did the lamb really follow her *everywhere* she would go? If it did, then why does it specifically say that it followed her to school one day? Perhaps we must not take "everywhere that she would go" literally.

And on and on it goes, but no matter where our questions take us, we're still left with the same undeniable facts: Mary *did* have a lamb. Its fleece was white, and it did go with her to school.

By the same token, no matter how much you want to deconstruct and question the Scriptures, you are still left with some unavoidable facts: There was a woman named Mary. She had a son named Jesus. He had many followers who wrote about Him and who spread His claim that He was the Son of God. He was referred to as the "Lamb of God." And He changed the course of human history.[9]

Tips for Reading: Context Is King

A bit of literary instruction would be fitting here. Have you ever heard a tidbit of information out of its entire context and then later heard it in its entirety and, as a result, saw it from a different perspective? For example, let's say you walk by your boss's office and hear, "Yes, I agree that [*your name here*] should definitely not be included." Prior to making the decision to jump out of your twenty-story office window, it would first behoove you to find out exactly what it is you are not to be included in. It may in fact be a plus not to be included in the next round of layoffs that were being discussed prior to your overhearing that one small phrase without context.

Too often, parts of the Bible are taken in pieces—outside of the context of the Bible in its entirety—and its message is distorted. Let's take the following extreme but salient example. Perhaps you are somewhat in despair regarding your current life situation and are looking for advice or encouragement from the Bible. You randomly open the Bible to Matthew 27:5b and read, "And he [Judas] went away and hanged himself" (NASB).

Thinking this can't possibly be the word of advice you were seeking, you turn randomly but hopefully to Luke 10:37b and read, "Then Jesus said, 'Go and do likewise'" (NASB).

Interpretation of Scripture is of utmost importance. You cannot and should not interpret every genre the Bible contains in the same way. Not all words strung together are created equally. Words have meaning of their own, but they have greater and varied meaning within the context of the surrounding words. The context contains the purpose and intent with which they were spoken or written.

This is not only true of the Holy Bible. Many things are only fitting and helpful considering their intended use. Product instructions for assembling a new bicycle are not amusing as a bedtime story. Likewise, the nursery rhyme "Old Mother Hubbard" is not helpful in assembling a new bicycle out of a box. Consider this traffic law: stop at all intersections with a red traffic light. Not entertaining or amusing, nor is it literary genius, but it is very beneficial to protect you and the other drivers and pedestrians on the road around you.

Just as each of these phrases should be considered in the context in which they were intended, various passages of the Bible should also be considered within the appropriate genre in which they were written. Parts of the Bible are written as history, while other parts are written as poetry. And they must be read as such.

In life, we can easily recognize the intent and purpose of most writing whether it comes in the newspaper or a children's book or out of a new appliance box. However, we are prone to take the Bible out of context. When reading Scripture, first consider the literary genre (historical narrative, poetry, etc.) and then read it within the context in which it was originally written.

Small Group or Bible Study Questions

Chapter 1: You Are Not Alone

1. What are the most difficult questions you ask God?

2. Describe what it's like to wrestle with doubt.

3. How has your relationship with your earthly father affected your relationship with God?

4. What's the connection between doubt and courage?

5. Reflect on or discuss the Kierkegaard quote "Life can only be understood backwards."

Chapter 2: Sliding on Ice

1. Describe your emotional state during a time of doubt.

2. Why do we see doubt as an enemy of faith?

3. How can doubt be a positive element in your life?

4. Examine or discuss the relationship between faith, certainty, and doubt.

5. Why do most people keep their doubt a secret?

6. How has this chapter changed your understanding of faith and doubt?

Chapter 3: Throwing Dishes at God

1. How have you processed those seasons of orientation, disorientation, and reorientation in your relationship with God? Talk about those seasons.

2. The story of Job often disturbs its readers. How do you feel about this visceral story?

3. Do you believe it's okay to vent at God like Job did? Why, or why not?

4. "Pain entered into, accepted, and owned can become poetry." How can we make that a reality in our lives?

Chapter 4: Demanding Evidence

1. What evidence for the existence of God do you find outside of the Bible?

2. Given the reality that Thomas saw Jesus perform miracles, why did he doubt?

3. Think of a time in your life when you felt isolated in doubt as John the Baptist did. Describe where you were when it happened.

4. Fill in the blank. All my doubts would cease if God would ______________________________.

5. Explain why miracles do not guarantee belief in God.

Chapter 5: Famous Doubters

1. Who are some of your heroes, and why do you admire them?

2. How do you relate to Mother Teresa's doubt about not feeling loved by God?

3. Mother Teresa, Martin Luther, or C. S. Lewis—whose doubt story surprised you the most? Why?

4. Talk about or write down some methods you've used to deal with doubt in your life. Which ones were most effective?

5. How do you feel about the way C. S. Lewis dealt with his anger toward God?

Chapter 6: Disappointed with God

1. Describe a time in your life when you felt God let you down.

2. What questions flood your mind when you are disappointed with God?

3. How do you process disappointment? What's your default response?

4. "There were others" has a haunting feel to it. How does this section of Hebrews 11 affect your view of faith?

5. Which five books of the Bible would you take to a deserted island? Explain the reason why you chose each book.

6. How can doubt strengthen your faith? What does it mean to "lean into doubt"?

Chapter 7: Searching for Certainty

1. Describe an area of cognitive dissonance in your life and how you attempt to resolve that tension.

2. How did modernism affect the Christian faith?

3. Discuss which worldview—modern or postmodern—is most compatible with Christianity.

4. How does our culture affect the way we think and live?

5. Explain the reasons why certainty sells across so many diverse cultures and religions.

6. How does certainty eliminate the need for faith?

Chapter 8: Letting Go of Certainty

1. How can clarity or certainty become an idol in our lives?

2. What are some of the ways we seek to achieve a sense of certainty? Think outside the box of religion.

3. How is our reason limited?

4. Are science and religion compatible? Explain your answer.

5. What does letting go of certainty look like for you?

Chapter 9: Burning Down the House

1. Describe the wide variety of foundations on which we build our lives.

2. How do you relate to the four layers laid out in this chapter? Describe the layers in your life.

3. List the essential elements of the Christian faith. Which ones are nonnegotiable?

4. Have you ever had doubts concerning your salvation? How have you dealt with those doubts?

5. Luther emphasized that the gospel is outside of you. What does that mean?

6. Christianity is a life experience, not a thought experiment. Discuss that statement.

Chapter 10: The Moon Is Round

1. If you have ever attended a Twelve Step group, describe that experience.

2. Where are some safe places you go to deal with doubt?

3. What aspects of Christianity trouble you? Do these aspects create doubt?

4. What emotions surround doubt? Why is shame most common?

5. Discuss new ways to befriend doubt.

6. Do you have any "the moon is round" reminders in your life? Write them down, or share them.

Notes

Chapter 1: You Are Not Alone

1. Paul C. Vitz, *Faith of the Fatherless: The Psychology of Atheism* (Dallas: Spence, 1999), 20, 26–31, 47–48, 104–7.

2. Søren Kierkegaard, *Journals IV A 164* (1843). Full quote is "It is perfectly true, as the philosophers say, that life must be understood backwards. But they forget the other proposition, that it must be lived forwards."

3. Julia Baird, "Doubt as a Sign of Faith," *New York Times*, September 25, 2014, www.nytimes.com/2014/09/26/opinion/julia-baird-doubt-as-a-sign-of-faith.html.

4. Paul Tillich, *Dynamics of Faith* (New York: HarperCollins, 2001), 117–18.

5. Jon Acuff, "The Scars Are Lighthouses," Stuff Christians Like, December 4, 2013, http://stuffchristianslike.net/2013/12/04/scars-lighthouses/.
6. Leighton Ford, *The Attentive Life: Discerning God's Presence in All Things* (Downers Grove, IL: InterVarsity, 2014), 79–80.

Chapter 2: Sliding on Ice

1. Kallistos Ware, *The Orthodox Way* (Crestwood, NY: St. Vladimir's Seminary Press, 1979), 16.
2. Os Guinness, *God in the Dark: The Assurance of Faith beyond a Shadow of Doubt* (Wheaton, IL: Crossway Books, 1996).
3. Lee Strobel, *The Case for Christ: A Journalist's Personal Investigation of the Evidence for Jesus* (Grand Rapids, MI: Zondervan, 1998), 9–19.
4. To be clear, I believe in the inerrancy of Scripture, but what I am referring to here is the naïve, wooden belief that our current manuscripts do not contain variances.
5. Bart Ehrman, *Misquoting Jesus: The Story behind Who Changed the Bible and Why* (New York: HarperCollins, 2009), 1–16.
6. Christopher Hitchens, *God Is Not Great: How Religion Poisons Everything* (New York: Twelve/Hachette, 2007), 1–13.
7. Peter Hitchens, *The Rage against God: How Atheism Led Me to Faith* (Grand Rapids, MI: Zondervan, 2010), 9–29.
8. Daniel Taylor, *The Skeptical Believer: Telling Stories to Your Inner Atheist* (St. Paul, MN: BOG Walk, 2013), 10–11.
9. Frederick Buechner, *Wishful Thinking: A Theological ABC* (San Francisco: Harper and Row, 1973), 20.

10. Hank Hanegraaff, *Christianity in Crisis* (Eugene, OR: Harvest, 1993), 66–71.

11. Gregory Boyd, *Benefit of the Doubt: Breaking the Idol of Certainty* (Grand Rapids, MI: Baker Books, 2013), 199.

12. Boyd, *Benefit of the Doubt*, 196.

13. Author paraphrase of David K. Clark, *Dialogical Apologetics: A Person-Centered Approach to Christian Defense* (Grand Rapids, MI: Baker Books, 1999), 18.

14. Clark, *Dialogical Apologetics*, 19.

15. Quoted in Christopher H. K. Persuad, *Famous People Speak about Jesus* (Xlibris Corporation, 2004), 181, www.xlibris.com.

16. Ware, *Orthodox Way*, 16.

Chapter 3: Throwing Dishes at God

1. Dan Allender, "The Hidden Hope in Lament," Allender Center, Seattle School of Theology and Psychology, June 2, 2016, http://theallendercenter.org/2016/06/hidden-hope-lament/.

2. Noted in Walter Brueggemann, *The Psalms and the Life of Faith* (Minneapolis, MN: Augsburg Fortress, 1995), 201, ebook.

3. Peter Kreeft, *Three Philosophies of Life: Ecclesiastes, Life as Vanity. Job, Life as Suffering. Song of Songs, Life as Love* (San Francisco: Ignatius, 1989), 91.

4. Mike Mason, *The Gospel According to Job: An Honest Look at Pain and Doubt from the Life of One Who Lost Everything* (Wheaton, IL: Crossway Books, 1994), 55–57.

5. Gary R. Habermas, *The Thomas Factor: Using Your Doubts to Draw Closer to God* (Nashville, TN: Broadman and Holman, 1999), 12.

6. Jennifer Michael Hecht, interview by Krista Tippett, "Speaking of Faith," American Public Media transcript, May 3, 2007.

7. Jerry Sittser, *A Grace Disguised: How the Soul Grows through Loss* (Grand Rapids, MI: Zondervan, 2004), 24–27.

8. Stephen Shortridge, *Deepest Thanks, Deeper Apologies: Reconciling Deeply Held Faith with Honest Doubt* (Brentwood, TN: Worthy, 2011), 8.

9. Kreeft, *Three Philosophies*, 88.

10. Ann O'Neill, "The Reinvention of Ted Turner," CNN, November 17, 2013, www.cnn.com/2013/11/17/us/ted-turner-profile/.

11. Sittser, *Grace Disguised*, 24–27.

12. Eugene H. Peterson, *First and Second Samuel* (Louisville, KY: Westminster John Knox, 1999), 144.

Chapter 4: Demanding Evidence

1. Madeleine L'Engle, *Two-Part Invention: The Story of a Marriage*, The Crosswicks Journal, bk. 4 (New York: HarperOne, 1989).

2. Bertrand Russell, *Bertrand Russell on God and Religion*, ed. Al Seckel (Amherst, NY: Prometheus Books, 1986), 11.

3. "George Müller, Orphanages Built by Prayer," Christianity.com, accessed April 5, 2017, www.christianity.com/church/church-history/church-history-for-kids/george-mueller-orphanages-built-by-prayer-11634869.html.

4. Lee Strobel's *The Case for Christ* and *The Case for the Resurrection* utilize this same evidential approach for proving the truthfulness of

Christianity. I highly recommend both books as tools for presenting Christ to the wary listeners you might encounter.

5. V. Raymond Edman, *The Disciplines of Life* (Eugene, OR: Harvest, 1982), 33.

6. Frederick Buechner, *Secrets in the Dark: A Life in Sermons* (New York: HarperCollins, 2006).

Chapter 5: Famous Doubters

1. C. S. Lewis, *A Grief Observed* (New York: HarperCollins, 2009), Kindle edition.

2. Frank Newport, "Mother Teresa Voted by American People as Most Admired Person of the Century," Gallup, December 31, 1999, www.gallup.com/poll/3367/mother-teresa-voted-american-people-most-admired-person-century.aspx?version=print.

3. Mother Teresa, *Come Be My Light: The Private Writings of the "Saint of Calcutta,"* ed. Brian Kolodiejchuk (New York: Doubleday Religion, 2007), 405.

4. Teresa, *Come Be My Light*, 291.

5. Teresa, *Come Be My Light*, 210.

6. Teresa, *Come Be My Light*, 288.

7. Chris R. Armstrong, "A History of Darkness," *Leadership Journal*, vol. 32, no. 4 (fall 2011), www.christianitytoday.com/le/2011/fall/historydarkness.html.

8. Teresa, *Come Be My Light*, 214.

9. Armstrong, "A History of Darkness."

10. Teresa, *Come Be My Light*, 214.

11. Armstrong, "A History of Darkness."

12. Dietrich Bonhoeffer, *Life Together: The Classic Exploration of Christian Community* (New York: HarperOne, 2009), 23.

13. Martin Marty, *Martin Luther: A Life* (New York: Penguin, 2008), Kindle edition, chap. 3.

14. Mark U. Edwards Jr., "Luther as Skeptic," *Christian Century*, November 17–24, 1999, www.religion-online.org/showarticle.asp?title=1493.

15. Erik H. Erikson, *Young Man Luther: A Study in Psychoanalysis and History* (New York: W. W. Norton, 1958), 58.

16. Armstrong, "A History of Darkness."

17. Armstrong, "A History of Darkness."

18. Armstrong, "A History of Darkness."

19. Marty, *Martin Luther*, 409–13.

20. Marty, *Martin Luther*, 417–24.

21. Marty, *Martin Luther*, 417–24.

22. M. J. Porter, "Wheaton College to Screen C. S. Lewis Documentary," *Daily Herald*, October 20, 2001, www.highbeam.com/doc/1G1-79384514.html.

23. "The Chronicles of Narnia," Box Office Mojo, accessed April 5, 2017, www.boxofficemojo.com/franchises/chart/?id=chroniclesofnarnia.htm.

24. Clyde S. Kilby, *The Christian World of C. S. Lewis* (Grand Rapids, MI: Eerdmans, 1995), 13.

25. C. S. Lewis, *Surprised by Joy: The Shape of My Early Life* (Orlando, FL: Harcourt, 1995), 132–33.

26. Kilby, *Christian World of C. S. Lewis*, 16.

27. Kilby, *Christian World of C. S. Lewis*, 18–19.

28. Lewis, *Surprised by Joy*, 221.

29. Lewis, *Surprised by Joy*, 222.

30. Kilby, *Christian World of C. S. Lewis*, 19–20.

31. Walter Hooper, in preface to *Lewis, Christian Reflections* (Grand Rapids, MI: Eerdmans, 1967), vii.

32. C. S. Lewis, *Mere Christianity* (London: Collins, 1952), 54–56.

33. Lewis, *Grief Observed*, chap. 2.

34. Lewis, *Grief Observed*, chap. 3.

35. Lewis, *Grief Observed*, chap. 22.

36. "H" is how Lewis referred to his wife, Joy Davidman, in the book *A Grief Observed*, which he originally wrote under the pseudonym N. W. Clerk.

37. Lewis, *Grief Observed*, chap. 27.

38. Lewis, *Grief Observed*, chap. 40.

39. Lewis, *Grief Observed*, chap. 28.

40. Lewis, *Grief Observed*, chaps. 15–16.

41. Lewis, *Mere Christianity*, 140.

42. Madeleine L'Engle, foreword to Lewis, *Grief Observed.*

Chapter 6: Disappointed with God

1. Michael Leunig, *The Prayer Tree* (New York: HarperCollins, 1992).

2. Eugene Peterson, *Reversed Thunder: The Revelation of John and the Praying Imagination* (New York: Harper Collins, 1991).

3. Stanley Hauerwas, *God, Medicine, and Suffering* (Grand Rapids, MI: Eerdmans, 1994).

4. Peter De Vries, *The Blood of the Lamb* (Chicago: University of Chicago Press, 1961).

5. Hauerwas, *God, Medicine, and Suffering*, 84.

6. I realize I will be criticized for insinuating that Jesus Christ doubted. I am aware of the theological problems that causes. Whether He doubted is not what I wish to argue. What is important is the question He asked. What He said is not up for debate, so just read His words and let them speak to you.

7. Quoted in Roger Lundin, *Emily Dickinson and the Art of Belief* (Grand Rapids, MI: Eerdmans, 2004), 3.

8. Hauerwas, *God, Medicine, and Suffering*, 84.

Chapter 7: Searching for Certainty

1. Leanne Payne, *The Healing Presence: Curing the Soul through Union with Christ* (Grand Rapids, MI: Baker Books, 1995), 183–84.

2. Peter Enns, "The Benefit of Doubt: Coming to Terms with Faith in a Postmodern Era," lecture, Asuza Pacific University, November 16, 2010, text available at http://peterennsonline.com/2010/11/24/the-benefit-of-doubt-coming-to-terms-with-faith-in-a-post-modern-era/.

3. Bradley Sickler, "Conflicts between Science and Religion," Internet Encyclopedia of Philosophy, February 11, 2009, accessed June 1, 2014, www.iep.utm.edu/.

4. Trevor Hart, *Faith Thinking: The Dynamics of Christian Theology* (Downers Grove, IL: InterVarsity, 1995), 29.

5. Ralph Allan Smith, "The Harmony of Faith and Reason: Why Believe the Bible?," Covenant Worldview Institute, 1998, www.berith.org/essays/apol/apol01.html.

6. John Cottingham, "Descartes, Doubt and Knowledge," iTunes University, Open University, June 13, 2011, www.open.edu/openlearn/history-the-arts/philosophy/exploring-philosophy?track=10.

7. Cottingham, "Descartes."

8. Smith, "Harmony."

9. Hart, *Faith Thinking*, 34.

10. Lesslie Newbigin, *Proper Confidence: Faith, Doubt, and Certainty in Christian Discipleship* (Grand Rapids, MI: Wm. B. Eerdmans, 1995), 25.

11. Enns, "Benefit of Doubt."

12. James Sire, *The Universe Next Door* (Downers Grove, IL: InterVarsity, 2009), 225.

13. Robertson Davies, *The Manticore* (New York: Penguin, 1972), 212.

14. Newbigin, *Proper Confidence*, 18.

15. Bart Ehrman, *Misquoting Jesus: The Story behind Who Changed the Bible and Why* (New York: HarperCollins, 2009), 1–16.

16. Daniel Taylor, *The Myth of Certainty: The Reflective Christian and the Risk of Commitment* (Downers Grove, IL: InterVarsity, 1999), 17–18, 152–53.

17. Jim Tour, interview by Ben Young, Houston, Texas, August 2009.
18. Dallas Willard, *Hearing God: Developing a Conversational Relationship with God* (Downers Grove, IL: InterVarsity, 2012), 283.

Chapter 8: Letting Go of Certainty

1. Mark Batterson, *In a Pit with a Lion on a Snowy Day: How to Survive and Thrive When Opportunity Roars* (Colorado Springs: Multnomah, 2016), 93.
2. Peter Enns, "The Benefit of Doubt: Coming to Terms with Faith in a Postmodern Era," lecture, Asuza Pacific University, November 16, 2010, text available at http://peterennsonline.com/2010/11/24/the-benefit-of-doubt-coming-to-terms-with-faith-in-a-post-modern-era/.
3. Daniel Taylor, *The Myth of Certainty: The Reflective Christian and the Risk of Commitment* (Downers Grove, IL: InterVarsity, 1999), 68.
4. James Spiegel, *The Making of an Atheist: How Immorality Leads to Unbelief* (Chicago: Moody, 2010).
5. Thomas Nagel, as quoted in J. Budziszewski, "The Second Tablet Project," First Things, June/July 2002, 28.
6. Richard P. Feynman, *Six Easy Pieces: Essentials of Physics Explained by Its Most Brilliant Teacher* (Reading, MA: Addison-Wesley, 1994), 138.
7. Quoted in Dean Nelson, "Why Certainty about God Is Overrated," *USA Today*, August 29, 2011, 7A.

8. *Blaise Pascal: Quotes and Facts*, ed. Blago Kirov, trans. Krasi Vasileva (CreateSpace Independent, 2016), 13.

9. Taylor, *Myth of Certainty*, 25.

10. Taylor, *Myth of Certainty*, 6.

11. Timothy Keller, *The Reason for God: Belief in an Age of Skepticism* (New York: Penguin, 2008).

12. Quoted in Nelson, "Why Certainty about God Is Overrated."

13. Quoted in Philip Yancey, *Reaching for the Invisible God: What Can We Expect to Find?* (Grand Rapids, MI: Zondervan, 2000), chap. 4.

14. Enns, "Benefit of Doubt."

Chapter 9: Burning Down the House

1. B. B. Warfield, quoted in Kenneth Boa and Robert M. Bowman Jr, *Faith Has Its Reasons: Integrative Approaches to Defending the Christian Faith* (Downers Grove, IL: InterVarsity, 2006), 84.

2. Letter from Martin Luther to Philip Melanchthon, Wartburg, August 1, 1521, Luther's *Works*, vol. 48, p. 282.

3. Dietrich Bonhoeffer, *Life Together: The Classic Exploration of Christian Community* (New York: HarperOne, 2009), 22.

4. Leanne Payne, *The Healing Presence: Curing the Soul through Union with Christ* (Grand Rapids, MI: Baker Books, 1995), 184.

5. *Daily Readings with Søren Kierkegaard* (Springfield, IL: Templegate, 1991), 34.

6. C. Stephen Evans addresses this concept in his book *Why Believe?: Reason and Mystery as Pointers to God* (Grand Rapids, MI: Eerdmans, 1996), Kindle edition, chap 8.

7. *The God Who Is There*, in *The Francis A. Schaeffer Trilogy: Three Essential Books in One Volume* (Wheaton, IL: Crossway, 1990).

Chapter 10: The Moon Is Round

1. Anne Lamott, *Plan B: Further Thoughts on Faith* (New York: Riverhead Books, 2006), 257.

2. Stephen King, *On Writing: A Memoir of the Craft* (New York: Simon & Schuster, 2010).

3. This note is for any of you who may hail from the ultra-conservative perspective and are leery of this leniency of the AA program to have grace for those who don't immediately and wholly accept the complete inerrancy of Scripture. Dr. James R. DeLoach is a lifelong godly mentor of mine. He is ninety-one years old, and he was a valiant warrior in the battle for inerrancy in the Southern Baptist Convention in the 1980s. He once told me that, over his lifetime, he has seen untold numbers of people come to faith in Christ through the AA program, in fact more so than through any other overtly evangelistic ministry.

4. Philip Yancey, "Faith and Doubt," 2009, accessed April 6, 2017, PhilipYancey.com, http://philipyancey.com/q-and-a-topics/faith-and-doubt.

5. John Bradshaw, *Bradshaw on the Family: A New Way of Creating Solid Self-Esteem* (Deerfield Beach, FL: Health Communications, 1988), 2–3.

6. Brennan Manning, *Ruthless Trust: The Ragamuffin's Path to God* (New York: HarperCollins, 2009), 104.

7. Robert M. Baird, "The Creative Role of Doubt in Religion," *Journal of Religion and Health* 19, no. 3 (fall 1980), 172–79, www.jstor.org/stable/27505571.

8. Martin Marty, *Martin Luther: A Life* (New York: Penguin, 2008), Kindle edition, 336–45.

9. Marty, *Martin Luther*, 336–45.

10. Bryan Chapell, *The Hardest Sermons You'll Ever Have to Preach: Help from Trusted Preachers for Tragic Times* (Grand Rapids, MI: Zondervan, 2011).

Appendix: Can You Trust the Bible?

1. Much of this chapter was influenced by Peter Kreeft, *Between Heaven and Hell* (Madison, WI: InterVarsity, 1982), 75–80.

2. "Much Apu about Nothing," *The Simpsons*, Fox Broadcasting Company (May 5, 1996).

3. Dr. Gregory Bahnsen used this line of argumentation in his epic 1985 debate with Dr. Gordon Stein, the former editor of *Skeptic Magazine*.

4. Helmut Koester, *History and Literature of Early Christianity*, vol. 2 (Philadelphia: Fortress, 1982), 16–17.

5. John A. T. Robinson, *Can We Trust the New Testament?* (Grand Rapids, MI: Eerdmans, 1977), 36.

6. *The Times* (London, England), www.soon.org.uk/page19.htm, referenced March 22, 2006.

7. *People's Gospel Hour*, "The Gospel Standard," vol. 44, no. 1 (September 1994): 17–18.

8. Michael Guillen, *Can a Smart Person Believe in God?* (Nashville, TN: Nelson Books, 2004), 2.

9. Adapted from Richard Pratt, "A Deconstruction of 'Mary Had a Little Lamb'" (lecture, Second Baptist Church, Houston, Texas, March 7, 2003).

Author Bio

Ben Young, DMin, is a teaching pastor at Second Baptist Church in Houston, Texas. He is also an adjunct professor at Houston Theological Seminary, and the author of seven books, including *Devotions for Dating Couples* and *Why Mike's Not a Christian.* Ben enjoys surfing and Brazilian jiu-jitsu.

www.benyoung.org

Other Books by Ben Young

Why Mike's Not a Christian:
Honest Questions about Evolution, Relativism, Hypocrisy, and More
by Ben Young

Common Grounds:
Conversations about the Things that Matter Most
by Ben Young and Glenn Lucke

The Ten Commandments of Dating:
Time-Tested Laws for Building Successful Relationships
by Ben Young and Dr. Sam Adams

Devotions for Dating Couples:
Building a Foundation for Spiritual Intimacy
by Ben Young and Dr. Sam Adams